Hints and signs of the coming King

Pictures of Jesus in the Old Testament

Kurt Strassner

DayOne

© Day One Publications 2010
First Edition 2010

Scripture quotations taken from the New American Standard Bible®, Copyright ©
1960, 1962, 1963, 1968, 1971, 1972, 1973, 1975, 1977, 1995 by The Lockman
Foundation Used by permission. (www.Lockman.org)

British Library Cataloguing in Publication Data available

ISBN 978-1-84625-208-2

Published by Day One Publications
Ryelands Road, Leominster, HR6 8NZ

☎ 01568 613 740
FAX: 01568 611 473
email—sales@dayone.co.uk
web site—www.dayone.co.uk
North American e-mail—usasales@dayone.co.uk
North American web site—www.dayonebookstore.com

Designed by Wayne McMaster and printed by Thomson Litho, East Kilbride

Dedication

As I prepared these chapters, it occurred to me that we can see Jesus pictured, not only in Old Testament lambs, arks, and manna, but also in the everyday lives and characters of fellow Christians (see 1 John 4:12, Phil. 2:5). For eleven years, my wife, Tobey, has been for me just such a portrait of Christlikeness. To her I dedicate this volume.

Endorsements

This book is an excellent evangelistic tool, particularly because it allows the eyes of our understanding to see Jesus through a number of "pictures" in the Old Testament. Whereas the Western world majors in abstract thought, here in Africa picture language is the way of communication, so I expect this book to find special appeal with us here. In that sense, we are very close to our Near Eastern neighbors. This book should be put into the hands of all those who need to hear the gospel afresh in this simple picture form. I cannot commend it too highly!

Conrad Mbewe, Pastor, Kabwata Baptist Church, Lusaka, Zambia

On the afternoon of Jesus's resurrection two of his disciples, walking from Jerusalem to Emmaus, enjoyed the privilege of a lifetime. Jesus joined them and gave them a journey-long personal seminar on what the Old Testament said about him. Kurt Strassner's Hints and Signs of the Coming King *provides an attractive guidebook to help us retrace that walk and discover for ourselves how the Old Testament points to Jesus. What's more, you can read it, enjoy it, and learn lifelong principles for your own Bible study—all in about the same length of time as a walk from Jerusalem to Emmaus. Enjoy the journey!*

Sinclair B. Ferguson, Senior Minister, First Presbyterian Church, Columbia, South Carolina, USA

Contents

Introduction

God seems to know that we human beings (or at least, many of us) are visual thinkers. To be sure, "faith comes from *hearing*"[1] and not primarily from *seeing* (Rom. 10:14–17). But often the "hearing" that God makes us privy to is of an almost visual manner. That is to say that the Lord seems, very often, to grant us what we might call word pictures—concrete, descriptive, often metaphoric ways of describing spiritual concepts: "Behold, *the Lamb* of God who takes away the sin of the world" (John 1:29); "All flesh is like *grass*" (1 Peter 1:24); "all our righteous deeds are like *a filthy garment*" (Isa. 64:6). And in Psalm 1:3 the man who fears the Lord is "like a *tree* firmly planted by streams of water, which yields its *fruit* in its season." Indeed, the list could go on, especially when we turn to the Gospels and find Jesus speaking in parables; the kingdom of heaven is like a mustard seed, a hidden treasure chest, a fishing net, and so on.

God often paints spiritual concepts with the bright colors and bold outlines of concrete illustrations and object lessons. In fact, sometimes we discover that it is not just Bible *teaching* that is metaphoric, but Bible *events* are as well! In other words, it is not just that God *says* things like "Behold, the Lamb of God who takes away the sin of the world" but sometimes he has worked out biblical history to *show* us (as in the Passover Lamb of Exod. 12).

To put it more simply, sometimes God painted word pictures through the lips of his prophets, apostles, and Son ("the

8

kingdom of heaven is *like* ..."); and sometimes, particularly in the Old Testament, he simply painted pictures in the form of real events, objects, and people. And often those real-life, real-time, touchable, historical pictures were portraits of the greatest of all subjects—his beloved Son. Not portraits of Jesus's face or form, of course; in that regard, the Bible is almost totally silent. We do not know a great deal about what Jesus looked (or looks) like, save that he was and is, indeed, fully human, and that he has telling nail prints in his hands and feet. But, although God has not given us much information about his Son's physical appearance, he has actually done better. All through the Bible, God has painted pictures of his Son's *work* on our behalf, portraits—in the form of various tangible objects and real-life events—that help us understand what Jesus is like, and what he has accomplished on our behalf. The Old Testament is packed full of these gospel portraits. In this book, we will consider just a handful of them. We will see that Jesus is ...

- an *ark* (Gen. 6–8) aboard which we may climb, escaping the flood waters of God's judgment;
- a *ram* (Gen. 22) willingly caught in the thicket of God's justice, so that he might set down his life in our place;
- our *Passover lamb* (Exod. 12), so that, when his blood is spread over our lives, the angel of death passes us by and we are saved from destruction;
- the bread that came down from heaven; the *manna* (Exod. 16) that feeds our hungry souls;

9

- a *tabernacle* in the wilderness (Exod. 25–30)—the one and only meeting place between God and man;
- a *bronze serpent* (Num. 21) lifted up on a pole so that all who look to him may be healed and live;
- the *lover* of our souls, our bridegroom, and the loveliest among ten thousand in the Song of Solomon;
- pictured in *the sign of Jonah*. For just as Jonah spent three days and nights in the belly of the fish and rose again, so the Son of Man spent three days and nights in the belly of the earth and rose again.

I hope you find as much pleasure and help in studying them as I have!

The ark of Noah

Now the earth was corrupt in the sight of God, and the earth was filled with violence. God looked on the earth, and behold, it was corrupt; for all flesh had corrupted their way upon the earth. Then God said to Noah, "The end of all flesh has come before Me; for the earth is filled with violence because of them; and behold, I am about to destroy them with the earth. "Make for yourself an ark of gopher wood ..."

Genesis 6:11–14

There are a great many lessons to be learned on board the ark of Noah. Genesis 6–9 surely teaches us about *the faithfulness of God*. Yes, God was angry with sinners. But it was he who gave them warning and who provided blueprints for an ark. And, in the midst of the flood, it was he who "remembered Noah" (8:1) and caused the floodwaters to recede. God initiated every single drop of good that spilled over from the flood. Genesis chapters 6–9 are about the faithfulness of God!

We must also say, however, that these famous chapters encourage us to imitate *the faithfulness of Noah*. For, although God initiated all the good that came through the flood, Noah still had to act and to do "according to all that God had commanded him" (6:22)—and so must we!

It should also be pointed out that the flood narrative in Genesis has something to teach us about *the history of the world*. There is not space in these pages for great detail, but let it suffice to say that if the world really was suddenly, catastrophically, and completely covered with the waters of a flood, that information must be factored into our scientific study of climate, plate tectonics, geology, fossil records, and so on. The flood was, literally, an earth-shaking event!

What is, however, most intriguing and momentous about the flood (indeed, most earth-shaking) is the way it foreshadowed the most important events in world history. What could be more momentous than a worldwide flood? The coming of God himself into the world in human flesh; the good news that sinners may be rescued from God's wrath, not only in body but also in soul; *the gospel of Jesus Christ!* These world-altering events are not only taught in the New Testament, they are also anticipated in the Old—especially as we consider the worldwide flood in Genesis 6–9. The flood and the ark are ancient portraits of the gospel, and in a number of different ways! First, the flood was:

A judgment upon sinners

The Genesis flood was not simply a meteorological chance event. No, the God who is absolutely sovereign over the weather ordained it (6:17). Why? Because the earth was filled with sin and with sinners. "[T]he LORD saw that the wickedness of man was great on the earth, and that every intent of the thoughts of his heart was only evil continually" (6:5). Therefore God said to Noah, "The end of all flesh has come before Me; for the earth is filled with violence because of them; and behold, I am about to destroy them with the earth" (v. 13).

The flood was a judgment upon sinners. I purposefully say upon *sinners*, and not just upon *sin*, for God did not simply destroy the people's sins; he destroyed the people themselves.

Men and women, boys and girls died in that flood. Look at them in your mind's eye—climbing, first to their second floors, then to their rooftops, and finally into the branches of the trees, hoping to escape. Picture them being washed away like seashells with the tide. Hear their screams echoing in your conscience. Why should we picture this? Because Genesis 6–9 records real, historical events. These things really happened, and, according to the apostle Peter, will happen again:

> ... by the word of God the heavens existed long ago and the earth was formed out of water and by water, through which the world at that time was destroyed, being flooded with water. But by His word the present heavens and earth are being reserved for fire, kept for the day of judgment and destruction of ungodly men.
>
> (2 Peter 3:5–7)

The flood, according to Peter, was a portrait of an even more significant judgment to come. Certainly God will keep his promise not to destroy the world again by means of water. But he *is* going to destroy the world again—by fire, and for the very same reasons given in the book of Genesis: the "destruction of ungodly men."

The situation is the same today as it was in the days of Noah. The earth is corrupt. "There is none righteous," Paul says in Romans 3:10, "not even one." Every single one of this world's inhabitants drags around a long record of sin and rebellion against God—you and I included. In fact, unless the Holy Spirit has taken up residence within us, it can be said of us, just as it was said of Noah's generation: "every intent of the thoughts of [our hearts is] only evil continually" (Gen. 6:5).

Does it sound far-fetched to say that *every* thought an unbelieving person has is evil? If "evil" only consists of things like lust, hate, and covetousness, then, no, it is not true that all man's thoughts are evil. Men and women do not always think in those ways. But the Bible teaches that the real definition of "evil" is simply ignoring God, living for ourselves, and doing what *we* think is best; it is therefore certainly true that the thoughts of an unsaved man or woman are "only evil continually." Men and women have either forgotten God or ignored him. They are trying to live without him. Even if people try to live moral lives of good citizenship, if they do so without faith in God and in his Son, they have committed the great evil of turning a blind eye toward their Maker! And that—apart from the redemption which is in Christ Jesus—is what all men, women, boys, and girls do. Some of us do so abruptly and angrily; others of us quietly and almost politely. But we have all turned away from him (Rom. 3:12).

So Genesis 6–9 really is an accurate parallel of our own day, and it is also a portrait of the gospel. "A portrait of *the gospel?*" you might ask. "It seems as if this first point has been more a portrait of the bad news than of the good." But good news never seems all that good unless we understand the bad news first.

Perhaps an accurate, sobering description of the *bad* news is what is absent in many a modern presentation of the *good* news! Maybe this is why our neighbors often have little time for the good news of forgiveness and love and eternal life in Jesus; they have yet to be convinced of the bad news! To many of our contemporaries, the good news seems more like a floating swimming-pool toy than the life-preserver it actually is. For if there is no flood coming—or, at least, if no one warns me about the coming flood—what is the use of climbing on board the ark? "I am fine just where I stand," say our friends and neighbors. And that is precisely where many of them will remain, only to be swept away someday without warning— unless we are brave and loving enough to tell them the bad news. No one will ever lay hold of God's *remedy* for sinners unless he or she understands God's *judgment* upon sinners. This brings us to our second heading:

A remedy for sinners

God provided a way of escape from the waters of the flood. Noah built an enormous ark that surely could have housed many people as well as animals. The ark was there for all Noah's neighbors to see. Additionally, as we will see later, Noah went about preaching to his neighbors, proclaiming a remedy for their sins.

The ark was a savior, a way of escape; in fact, the *only* way of escape. No doubt many of Noah's contemporaries, as the waters began to rise, attempted to rescue themselves. Surely the roofs and trees of every village in the world were full on that terrible day. Some people probably tried desperately to turn various household containers into life rafts. Others, perhaps, fled to the heights of the mountains. But none of these remedies availed. For even the world's highest mountain tops were submerged by the waters of the flood (7:19). The deluge was simply too much for these various makeshift solutions. What was needed was a giant ship—the ark of Noah, designed by God himself. The ark was the only way of escape.

A way of escape for sinners—but only one way of escape. Does that sound familiar? Has God provided a remedy for sinners today? Has he provided a way of escape from the fires that will soon engulf the earth? Yes, he has. He has sent his Son to die the death that we sinners deserve. He has sent his Son to withstand, on our behalf, the floodwaters of his wrath. He has sent his Son to be, as it were, our ark. Is that not wonderful news? God has not left us without a life raft or rescue boat. Jesus has come, just like Noah's ark, perfectly fitted to be our salvation. The ark met every requirement to withstand a flood (6:14–17)—its construction was sturdy, its seams were sealed with pitch, its size was enough to accommodate all on board. In the same way Jesus, by his sinless life, his sacrificial death, and his resurrection from the grave, has made every provision for *us*. He has perfectly fulfilled God's blueprint. He, like Noah's ark, is all we need!

In addition, it must be said that Jesus is not only all we *need*, but also all we *have*. He, like Noah's ark, is the one and only remedy that will hold up on the Day of Judgment. As it must have been in the days of Noah, so it will be on that last day. Men and women will attempt all sorts of do-it-yourself remedies: "But Lord, I was a good person"; "Lord, I went to church every week"; "Lord, the pastor told me that if I just walked down the aisle and filled out that little card, everything would be fine"; "Lord, if you let me in I will promise never to sin again. You'll see. Just please let me in." But these self-help solutions will be of no avail. As in the days of Noah, those who have spent a lifetime ignoring God's remedy will find their last-second solutions overturned like rotten driftwood. For "*I* am the way, and the truth, and the life," says Jesus in John 14:6; "no one comes to the Father but through *Me*."

There is only one remedy for sinners—Jesus, our ark. But, just as in the days of Noah, there is plenty of room for more passengers, even today. If you have never yet experienced the forgiveness of sins, if you do not have the assurance that you will be safe with Jesus when God's judgment once again comes upon the earth, there is still room to mount the gangway with Jesus. His death is sufficient to assuage all of God's wrath against you. But will you climb aboard?

To help persuade you to do so, and to encourage you to bring a great many others with you, consider, finally:

A message to sinners

Noah was more than just a ship-builder: the apostle Peter calls him "a preacher of righteousness" (2 Peter 2:5). In other words, it would appear that, during all those long, hard years of building the ark, Noah also dedicated himself to preaching. Preaching what? The Bible does not tell us exactly. But surely we are right to presume that, as Noah built his ship, he said to himself, "I can't keep this news to myself. I have to get out and tell my neighbors that God is angry with their sins; that a great flood is coming; that they are all destined to perish; but that, if they will repent, and if they will climb aboard this ark, they will be saved. I cannot just build this boat; I must point people to the boat, too. I cannot just be concerned about me and my family being rescued; I have to preach! I have to spread the news—both bad and good!"

Whether anyone listened or not, Noah committed himself to being "a preacher of righteousness." And so must each of us! Can we be content to know about the ark, to climb aboard it ourselves, to get our families safely up the ramp and then to hunker down and forget that the flood of God's judgment is coming upon our neighbors?

Imagine you had lived in the city of New Orleans when Hurricane Katrina hit. Picture yourself paddling safely through the devastated Ninth Ward in your fishing boat. Imagine seeing, as the water rises, people hacking through their roofs and scrambling desperately to higher ground. Would it not be criminal to have the means of rescue and not offer a way of escape? Would it not be criminal just to paddle silently by with empty seats in your boat? And would it not have been criminal for Noah, knowing about the imminent danger, to have withheld the warning from his neighbors? Then why is it that I am so often remiss in sharing the only way of rescue with my neighbors and family members? Is not that kind of silence criminal?

If the wages of sin is death, if eternal judgment is coming, if personal faith in Jesus is the only means of escape—with whom ought *you* to be sharing the good news in the coming week? How ought you to be strategizing to provide yourself with opportunities to speak for Jesus? Or, as Peter asks in 2 Peter 3:11, "Since all these things are to be destroyed in this way, what sort of people ought you to be …"?

Reflect on these points

1. The Bible continually teaches that there is nothing inherently good within fallen mankind (see Gen. 6:5; Rom. 3:10–18; Isa. 64:6). But, outwardly, people seem to do good things all the time. What are some inner, heart realities that help us understand why Isaiah could say that even our "righteous deeds" are "like a filthy garment"?

2. Are you tempted to rely upon makeshift solutions to your sin problem? Promises to do better? Pledges to try harder? Religious attainments or church affiliation? Think deeply about where your hope for eternity truly lies. Are you on board the ark—or clinging desperately (but hopelessly) to a piece of religious driftwood? Whom are you actually trusting for eternal salvation—Jesus or yourself?

3. Surely we, like Noah, should be "preachers of righteousness." Make a list of a few people with whom you ought to be sharing the good news in the days ahead. Pray for them regularly, and take the opportunities God puts before you!

The ram in
the thicket

Now it came about after these things, that God tested Abraham, and said to him ... "Take now your son, your only son, whom you love, Isaac, and go to the land of Moriah, and offer him there as a burnt offering on one of the mountains of which I will tell you" ... Abraham built the altar ... and bound his son Isaac and laid him on the altar, on top of the wood. Abraham stretched out his hand and took the knife to slay his son. But the angel of the LORD called to him from heaven and said ... "Do not stretch out your hand against the lad ... now I know that you fear God, since you have not withheld your son, your only son, from Me." Then Abraham raised his eyes and looked, and behold, behind him a ram caught in the thicket by his horns; and Abraham went and took the ram and offered him up for a burnt offering in the place of his son.

Genesis 22:1–2, 9–13

There can be little doubt that the events of Genesis 22 were a most severe test of Abraham's faith. God wanted to see (and to allow Abraham to see) whether or not Abraham would maintain his faith if God took away his earthly everything. There is, therefore, much in Abraham's testing that speaks to us, too. Would I trust God if he asked me, like Abraham, to give up that which is most precious? Would I still serve God if, like Job, I lost my earthly all? Those are questions each of us must ponder, and Genesis 22 powerfully helps us to do so.

There was, however, a second reason for Abraham's test. God ordained the testing of Abraham, not only to force us to ask ourselves the same hard questions Abraham had to answer, but also to paint for us another picture of Jesus and of his gospel. For God, in giving us his only Son, put himself through exactly the same testing he required of Abraham. If you read Genesis 1–14 you may begin to connect the dots between Genesis 22 and the cross of Christ. The mosaic of the crucifixion story that God pieces together in these verses is marvelous and beautiful, and crystal clear. The parallels are amazing. Let's look at three profound portraits of the gospel from this chapter of Genesis.

Abraham's sacrifice

What a test Abraham faced! "Take now your son," God told him in verse 2, "your only son, whom you love, Isaac, and go to the land of Moriah, and offer him there as a burnt offering." This was an astonishing request, not least because Isaac had been a miracle child, born to Abraham and Sarah when they were well into their "retirement years." Further, Isaac had been born as a direct promise from on high (ch. 18). And now the same God who promised and gave this miracle child was going to take him away in the prime of his youth?

It was a sore test, and one we should all contemplate. Would we, like Abraham, still serve God if he took away a child, a spouse, or a parent? But there is something else to see when we look into the tormented face of Abraham. Yes, we should hope to see, in his face, a reflection of the kind of faith that we would all like to have. But we should also see a portrait of our heavenly Father, who also willingly gave up his only Son!

Upon reading Genesis 22, one cannot help noticing that the

circumstances of Abraham's sacrifice were almost identical to those of the heavenly Father as he prepared to sacrifice his own Son on the cross. Both Jesus and Isaac were only sons.[1] Both, too, were to be offered up as sacrifices in the mountains of Moriah (v. 2). If you look up the name "Moriah" in a concordance, you will find that this was the spot where, centuries later, David built up Israel's capital city (Jerusalem), and where Solomon built God's temple. In the very same hill country where Abraham was to sacrifice his son, God himself offered *his* only Son.

Furthermore, we should be struck by the fact that Isaac was to be sacrificed by his very own father. Isaac was not going to die of natural causes, or as the result of some accident. Nor was it a servant who would wield the sacrificial knife (v. 5). Abraham himself was to "offer him there" (v. 2). This, too, is a picture of the gospel and of the heavenly Father. Jesus did not die by accident. It was not simply that the rising tide of political opposition got to him before his time. And, though the Jewish leaders forced the issue and the Roman soldiers drove in the nails, Isaiah reminds us that, just as God had instructed Abraham so long before, the Father himself was, ultimately, to offer the sacrifice! "He was crushed for our iniquities" (Isa. 53:5), and it was *the LORD*"who "was pleased to crush Him" (53:10).

The author of Hebrews reminds us that both Abraham and the heavenly Father approached the sacrifice in the land of Moriah with the same hope, too. Abraham was able to go up that mountain with his only son because he believed that "God is able to raise people even from the dead" (Heb. 11:17–19). In other words, he said to himself, "It's OK. Isaac's life was a miracle in the first place. Surely God can work another miracle and make him alive again. After all, God did promise that, through Isaac, our little family would be a blessing to all the nations of the earth, so surely this cannot be the end." Abraham knew that God could raise the dead. And God, of course, also knew that about himself. So it was that, just like Abraham, God laid his Son on the altar in the certainty of the resurrection!

The parallels are striking: an only son, sacrificed by his father, in the mountains of Moriah, in the hope of the resurrection! There can be little doubt that God intends us to see Genesis 22 as a kind of dress rehearsal for the great sacrifice that has been made for us in Jesus! God wants us to read Genesis 22 and see, not only Abraham's great sacrifice, but also his own!

God gave *his only Son*—for you! Think about what that means. Think about what it is like, or must be like, to lose a child. Think about what it signifies that God did so, willingly—for you! "We would almost think," Sinclair Ferguson has often said, "that God loves us more than he loves his only Son."[2] We know that this is not true, for God loves his Son more than anything else. But it almost sounds true, because God actually gave his only Son for us! If you can feel even a fraction of the weight of that sentence, can you keep from embracing this God one moment longer?

How great is the Father's love for us! But we should also see, reflected in the events of Genesis 22, just what *the Son* has done for us, too:

Isaac's obedience

Surely Isaac's heart was just as full as his father's, especially as we approach verse 8. In verse 7, Isaac had asked an honest and innocent question: "Behold, the fire and the wood, but where is the lamb for the burnt offering?" Perhaps Abraham's answer in verse 8 comforted him somewhat. But by the time we get to verse 9, Abraham was removing the bundle of wood from Isaac's back, arranging it for the offering, and placing Isaac himself on the altar!

Do not fail to notice that *Isaac* was the one carrying the wood (v. 6)! Notice also that, for there to have been enough wood to sustain a fire that would consume an entire human body, it must have been no small amount. What that means, of course, is that Isaac must have been no little boy. Surely he was at least into his teenage years, if not older, when these events took place. This was not Abraham manhandling a seven-year-old and tying him down to the altar; Isaac was a sturdy young man. Add to that the fact that, by this point, Abraham was well over a hundred years old, and it becomes clear that Isaac *allowed* his father to place him on the altar!

By the time they arrived at verse 9, Isaac knew very well what was happening. The lamb that God was providing was to be himself! And, strong enough as he was to carry a large bundle of wood up the side of a mountain, surely Isaac would have been strong enough to overpower a hundred-plus-year-old man! Yet that is not what we read. Instead we read that "Abraham built the altar … and arranged the wood, and bound his son Isaac and laid him … on top of the wood" (v. 9). It cannot be doubted that Isaac went up onto that killing stone knowing full well what was happening—and yet allowing it willingly.

Is Isaac's obedience not an eye-catching sketch of the gospel of Jesus? Yes, Jesus's heart was heavy—just like Isaac's must have been. He even prayed that God might allow the cup of suffering to pass him by (Luke 22:42). But, very quickly, he reminded his Father that he was willing to be laid on the altar: "not My will, but Yours be done." Jesus submitted to God's plan, just like Isaac! There is a sense in which, like Isaac, he could have wriggled himself free. He could have "come down from the cross," as the scoffers challenged him to do in Mark 15:32. He could have called "more than twelve legions of angels" (Matt. 26:53) to rescue him. But he didn't. Just like Isaac so many years before, he stayed bound to the altar—bound to the cross—that day in the land of Moriah.

Why did he do it? Why did Jesus not come down from the cross? Surely one reason was because he loved people like you and me, and because our sin necessitated that he die for us. Our need for forgiveness—and his loving desire to provide it—held him to the cross. But there was an even greater reason he stayed hanging on that tree, a greater love that kept him from calling twelve legions of angels to rescue him. It was, it would seem, the same reason why Isaac did not wrestle himself free of his father's grip in Genesis 22: because he loved, trusted, and wanted to honor his father. That is why Isaac allowed himself to be bound on that altar, and why he stayed there once the knots were tied. And that is certainly why Jesus went to the cross and did not come down when he so easily could have—because he loved, trusted, and wanted to honor his Father!

The apostle Paul makes this clear in Philippians 2:8 when he tells us that Jesus "humbled Himself by becoming obedient to the point of death, even death on a cross." Obedience! That is why Jesus prayed, "not My will, but Yours be done." That is why he did not come down from the cross. That is why he did not empty heaven of its angels that day. Because he loved his Father and longed, more than anything else, to obey him!

We might put it this way: it was Jesus's consistent, never-failing love for and obedience to his Father that made him fit to *go* to the cross, as a sinless sacrifice, to die for our sins. And it was Jesus's consistent, never-failing love for and obedience to his Father that *kept* him on the cross, too! Praise God for the obedience of an "only son"—pictured wonderfully in the son of Abraham and fulfilled perfectly in the Son of God!

Exquisite as Isaac's obedience was, however, we have not yet reached the end of Genesis 22. The story only gets better—and more gospel-like—as we look, finally, at:

God's substitute

The similarities between Isaac and Jesus—conspicuous as they are—do not continue beyond verse 9. For, just as Abraham was about to bring the knife down across his son's throat (v. 10), and as Isaac was about to give his life as a willing sacrifice, God called off the test. Abraham had proven his faithfulness to his God. He had not withheld from the Lord his only son, whom he loved (v. 12). And so the Lord allowed him to stay his hand. "Then Abraham raised his eyes and looked, and behold, behind him a ram caught in the thicket by his horns; and Abraham went and took the ram and offered him up for a burnt offering in the place of his son" (v. 13).

How merciful God is! What grace he offered both Abraham and Isaac that day! Seemingly out of nowhere (but all according to God's gracious plan) there was a substitute for young Isaac. The knife was held above his head, and yet it came down upon another. Certain death was his portion, and yet the death befell another, in his place.

There is, perhaps, no simpler portrait of the gospel in all Scripture. For you and I, because of our sin, have lain in exactly the same place as Isaac. "For the wages of sin is death" (Rom. 6:23). Therefore, in our unbelieving states, we had (whether we realized it or not) a knife always hanging above our heads. We never knew when it would come down, when our time would be up and our sins would be avenged. Perhaps you are still lying on that killing stone today because you have not come to Christ. Apart from Christ, we walk constantly on the very precipice of hell, ever ready to slip in without a moment's notice. Yet the gospel informs us that God has taken Jesus, like the ram in verse 13, and "offered him up ... in the place of" sinners like us! Jesus has died the death that we deserve, in our place!

Again, the similarities between Isaac and Jesus end in verse 9. For God spared Isaac, yet he "did not spare His own Son, but delivered Him over for us all" (Rom. 8:32). God did not spare his own Son, but instead allowed him to be caught in the thicket of Jewish jealousies and Roman politics, of Judas Iscariot's deception, of that crown of thorns, and of those nails which, like the wild bush in Genesis 22, held the sacrifice in place.

Make no mistake, Jesus was caught there willingly. He knew exactly what was at stake. He understood that he was the ram—and he gladly allowed himself to be caught and offered up for us! Jesus is our ram, willingly caught in the thicket of God's wrath against sin, and laying down his life in the place of so many Isaacs like you and me.

Have you received him as your ram? If so, then Genesis 22 is another encouragement toward a grateful heart. But so many people attempt to wriggle their way out from under the knife on their own—perhaps even you who read these pages. You may be convincing yourself, falsely, that "God surely won't bring that knife down on me. I haven't done anything *that* bad." Or you may be salving your conscience by saying, "God would never kill anybody. After all, God is love." Perhaps you hope to talk God out of the punishment you have incurred by promising to do better and try harder. But all the while—as you come up with reason after reason to believe the devil's lie that, even though you have sinned, you "will not surely die"—there is "a ram caught in the thicket," a substitute for sinners, a God-ordained way of escape: Jesus who was "offered … up … in the place of" sinners! Why not turn around then, with Abraham, and lay hold of him?

Reflect on these points

1. In addition to the gospel parallels in Genesis 22, there are personal parallels. Have you faced a severe loss, as Abraham had to face, or an extreme call to submission like Isaac? How should a Christian respond in such cases? What is the appropriate way to ask God "why?" or "how long?" Consider Abraham and Isaac's faith, especially as described in Hebrews 11.

2. Are there other "substitute" pictures in the Scriptures like that of the ram in Genesis 22? Look for this theme as you daily read your Bible. For a few examples, see Genesis 44, Leviticus 16, Matthew 27, and Philemon 18.

3. There were other sacrifices made in the hills of Moriah. Use a concordance or online Bible tool to research "the threshing floor of Ornan the Jebusite" (2 Chr. 3:1), a parcel of ground that King David bought in Moriah. How do the various events that took place there also picture Jesus?

The Passover lamb

Speak to all the congregation of Israel, saying, "On the tenth of this month they are each one to take a lamb for themselves ... a lamb for each household ... Your lamb shall be an unblemished male a year old; you may take it from the sheep or from the goats. You shall keep it until the fourteenth day of the same month, then the whole assembly of the congregation of Israel is to kill it at twilight. Moreover, they shall take some of the blood and put it on the two doorposts and on the lintel of the houses in which they eat it. They shall eat the flesh that same night ... and you shall eat it in haste—it is the LORD's Passover. For I will go through the land of Egypt on that night, and will strike down all the firstborn in the land of Egypt, both man and beast; and against all the gods of Egypt I will execute judgments—I am the LORD. The blood shall be a sign for you on the houses where you live; and when I see the blood I will pass over you, and no plague will befall you to destroy you when I strike the land of Egypt.

Exodus 12:3, 5–8, 11–13

One of the most striking of all the Old Testament's gospel portraits is summed up by the apostle Paul's words in 1 Corinthians 5:7: "Christ our Passover also has been sacrificed." *Jesus* is the Passover, or Passover lamb. And, says Paul, Jesus is "*our* Passover"! All that the Passover symbolized for the Old Testament saints—deliverance from bondage, God's provision and care, the need for blood sacrifice, and rescue from certain death—Christ is for his people today! The Passover, then, was a grand and beautiful work of art, painted by the hand of God, and portraying the sacrifice and salvation given to us in Jesus!

To help us understand just what we have been given in "Christ our Passover," we need to look more closely at the Old Testament Passover observance itself from Exodus 12. And to appreciate the picture God paints in Exodus 12, we need to remember the larger context. So let's begin with a little background.

Israel's exodus from Egypt

The year was 1446 BC and the Lord's people, Israel, had been in captivity in the land of Egypt for 430 years (see Exod. 12:41). But God, being rich in mercy and compassion, had spoken to Moses from a burning bush, saying,

> I have surely seen the affliction of My people who are in Egypt, and have given heed to their cry because of their taskmasters, for I am aware of their sufferings. So I have come down to deliver them from the power of the Egyptians, and to bring them up from that land to a good and spacious land, to a land flowing with milk and honey, to the place of the Canaanite and the Hittite and the Amorite and the Perizzite and the Hivite and the Jebusite. Now, behold, the cry of the sons of Israel has come to Me; furthermore, I have seen the oppression with which the Egyptians are oppressing them. Therefore, come now, and I will send you to Pharaoh, so that you may bring My people, the sons of Israel, out of Egypt.
>
> (Exod. 3:7–10)

After some initial misgivings and objections, Moses did obey the Lord and go to Pharaoh, king of Egypt, delivering God's message to him: "Let My people go, that they may serve Me in the wilderness" (Exod. 7:16). But Pharaoh did not listen to the Lord's command. Instead, he hardened his heart and God, therefore, redeemed the people of Israel from Pharaoh's grip "with an outstretched arm and with great judgments" (Exod. 6:6).

The Lord sent great plagues on the land of Egypt (see Exod. chs. 7–12). First, the Nile River and all the waters of Egypt turned to blood. Then the land was overrun, successively, by frogs, gnats, and flies. But still Pharaoh would not let the people go. So the Lord sent pestilence, killing much of Egypt's livestock. Next came a plague of boils, or great sores, on both man and beast. Then there was a tremendous hail storm, followed by the invasion of millions of locusts which destroyed all the crops of Egypt. Yet Pharaoh's heart remained hard. So God sent three days of supernatural darkness—a darkness that could be felt and that not even a lamp or a fire could penetrate. Moses wrote that "They did not see one another, nor did anyone rise from his place for three days" (Exod. 10:23).

Still, despite all these terrors, Pharaoh would not let the people go. So the Lord prepared to unleash a tenth, final, and most devastating plague upon the land of Egypt: "About midnight," he said,

> I am going out into the midst of Egypt, and all the
> firstborn in the land of Egypt shall die, from the firstborn

of the Pharaoh who sits on his throne, even to the firstborn of the slave girl who is behind the millstones; all the firstborn of the cattle as well. Moreover, there shall be a great cry in all the land of Egypt, such as there has not been before and such as shall never be again. But against any of the sons of Israel a dog will not even bark, whether against man or beast, that you may understand how the LORD makes a distinction between Egypt and Israel.

(11:4–7)

Such was the hardness of Pharaoh's cruel heart. And such was God's commitment to set his people free from Pharaoh's cruel yoke.

The Passover

Before God sent this last curse, however, he gave very specific instructions as to how his people might avoid the plague of death. The way of escape from that night of terror, he told them, was through the blood of a lamb (12:1–13). Only by spreading the lamb's blood over their individual doorways could the people of Israel be delivered from death. Indeed, when God saw the blood on a doorframe, he would *pass over* that house and not execute his judgment upon it. Thus it was called the night of the Passover.

What a night it must have been! That very night God brought vengeance upon the Egyptians and led his people, finally, out of their slavery. Further, he commanded the

Israelites (12:14) never to forget this night, but to remember it in an annual memorial observance. So, as the years went by, the faithful celebrated this same Passover meal every spring, looking back on what God had done, but also looking forward in the hope that someday a Messiah (or, in Greek, a "Christ") would come to deliver God's people again. Many of them, in fact, anticipated that the Messiah would come on the very day God had delivered them from Egypt so long before—on the day of Passover!

An unblemished lamb

Nearly 1500 years went by, and the faithful among God's people were still celebrating the Passover and awaiting the Messiah. Around the year AD 30, as they approached this special time of remembrance and anticipation, there was quite a buzz around Jerusalem about a man named Jesus of Nazareth: "Could this be the Messiah that we have all been waiting for?" the people gossiped among themselves. "Did he not say to us, 'The Spirit of the Lord is upon Me, because He anointed Me to preach the gospel to the poor. He has sent Me to proclaim release to the captives, and recovery of sight to the blind, to set free those who are oppressed, to proclaim the favorable year of the Lord' [Luke 4:18–19]? Maybe *this* is the favorable year of the Lord! I wonder if he will show up in Jerusalem for Passover. They say the Messiah will appear at Passover and deliver us, just as our forefathers were delivered in Moses's day. Maybe this is the year; and maybe this Jesus is the deliverer!"

Amid all the excitement, the tenth day of the first month finally arrived—the day upon which the Israelites were to set aside the unblemished Passover lamb as God had directed in Exodus 12:3–5. Thousands upon thousands of religious pilgrims had arrived in Jerusalem for the Passover celebration, and many of them were out in the streets as Jesus entered the city, riding like a king on the foal of a donkey. His arrival was a crowded and much anticipated event. The great prophet (and perhaps the Messiah!) was coming to town—Jesus, who had healed the lame and raised the dead; who had taught the masses with an accuracy and authority they had never before known; who, under all the tests and temptations of the experts in the law, had kept his balance perfectly; "who committed no sin, nor was any deceit found in His mouth" (1 Peter 2:22).

That day, God's portrait—and its fulfillment—were on display for those with eyes to see. On the very day that the unblemished, spotless lamb of the Passover was to be brought into the city and set aside for sacrifice, God also brought in and set aside his own Lamb. On that tenth day of the first month of the Jewish calendar, the Lord brought his own sacrifice to the festival—one who was "unblemished" by sin!

Here is one reason why Paul called Jesus "our Passover." Like that lamb so long before, he was unblemished and spotless, and therefore qualified to be the blood sacrifice that we need. Before Jesus's blood was ever shed, it was clear (to the few who saw through the eyes of faith) that, because he was blameless,

Jesus was indeed fit to become our great and final Passover Lamb! Is that clear to *you*? Have you recognized that Jesus is everything that you are not—unblemished and spotless? Have you marveled at and loved his purity? And have you received him as the unblemished sacrifice for your sins?

"When I see the blood, I will pass over you"

The Passover lamb was to be selected, examined, and set aside on the tenth day of the month. But, according to Exodus 12:6, it was not until the fourteenth day that "the whole assembly of the congregation of Israel" was to take the lamb and "kill it at twilight." That night, after having slaughtered their lambs, individuals and families were to roast the meat and eat it together in individual households. This was the great culmination of the Passover festival. So, as we look forward again into the New Testament Gospels, we find Jesus and his disciples, right around dusk, in the upper room of a house in Jerusalem, celebrating the Passover meal together according to God's commandment.

There was other symbolism involved in the meal. Jesus told his disciples that the unleavened bread of the Passover supper was a symbol of his body, broken for them. After supper, he took the customary chalice of Passover wine and informed them that it too was a portrait—of his blood poured out for the forgiveness of sins. But then something both tragic and wonderful occurred.

During the middle of supper, Judas Iscariot rose from his seat and walked out of the room. Why the abrupt exit?

Because, traitor that he was, Judas had already made arrangements with the religious leaders in Jerusalem to help them get rid of their Nemesis. So he left the Passover meal to report Jesus's whereabouts to Caiaphas, the high priest, who, in his plot to kill Jesus, had said, "it is expedient ... that one man die for the people, and that the whole nation not perish" (John 11:50). How right he was, without ever realizing it! So it was that, on the very night of the Passover, Jesus was handed over, like the Passover lamb, to be slain by (and on behalf of) "the congregation of Israel" (Exod. 12:6).

The soldiers who were charged with Jesus's execution twisted together a horrific crown of thorns and jammed it onto Jesus's head so that blood gushed out freely. They laid his body across two wooden posts, not unlike the doorposts upon which the blood of the Passover lamb was to be spread (Exod. 12:7), and nailed his body in place. And, as we watch, with our mind's eye, the blood from Jesus's head, hands, and feet dripping down those wooden posts, we see Exodus 12 being replayed, in amazing detail, before us. All the particulars—the unblemished sacrifice, the blood, the wooden posts—were repeated at and fulfilled in the cross of Christ!

Most importantly, the promise of safety in the face of death (which was so crucial on that first Passover night) was also repeated at and fulfilled in the cross of Christ. The blood of the lamb, in Exodus 12, was displayed publicly on the doorframes of people's homes so that the wrath of God would not fall on the Israelites. "[W]hen I see the blood I will pass over you," God said (Exod. 12:13). And the apostle Paul reminds us that Jesus, in the same way, was "*displayed publicly* as a propitiation [or wrath-absorbing sacrifice] in His blood" (Rom. 3:25). It is the same magnificent picture! When God sees the blood of Jesus—publicly displayed at the cross, and spread over the lives of those who believe—he passes over them so that death (in this case, eternal death in hell) does not overtake them.

The purpose of the Passover lamb has its ultimate fulfillment in Jesus! The Passover was a majestic, terrible, and glorious example of God's commitment to stay his hand when a blood sacrifice had been made and believed upon. And, therefore, the Passover was a majestic, terrible, and glorious portrait of Jesus and the gospel! This is why Paul says in 1 Corinthians 5:7 that "Christ our Passover also has been sacrificed"! Just like the children of Israel on that terrible night of death in Egypt, *we* have a way of escape. Just like them, *we* have a Passover Lamb! But also just like them, we must apply the blood of the Lamb to our lives personally. No Israelite was saved just because he or she was an Israelite. Each Israelite had to believe God's promise and apply the blood to his or her doorposts. The same can be said of religious people today. No one will ever be saved simply through having been brought up to be religious. The only way of escape on the Day of Judgment will be the blood of the unblemished Lamb, consciously spread over the life of a believer. And when God sees that we have, by faith, spread the blood of the Lamb across the doorposts of our lives, he passes over us, and the plague of eternal death does not befall us!

Reflect on these points

1. The lamb was not the only portrait of Jesus God painted in the Passover. Jesus reminds us that the bread served at the supper also points to his sacrifice on our behalf (see Matt. 26, for example). Think about why it was important that the bread of the Passover (and, subsequently, the Lord's Supper) was to be unleavened. See especially 1 Corinthians 5. What does this symbol teach us about Jesus?

2. Many Westerners, Jew and Gentile alike, are somewhat familiar with the Exodus story, especially as it has been portrayed in various film versions. How could you use the Passover as an evangelistic talking point with an unbelieving friend?

3. The Israelites were not passed over on the night of death simply because they were Israelites, but rather because they specifically applied the blood to their doorposts. The same is true for churchgoers today: we are not saved merely because we are churchgoers. So how can we tell—from the way we pray, talk about, and understand our Christian lives—if we are really relying on the blood of Jesus and not simply on our religious activity?

The manna
from heaven

So it came about at evening that the quails came up and covered the camp, and in the morning there was a layer of dew around the camp. When the layer of dew evaporated, behold, on the surface of the wilderness there was a fine flake-like thing, fine as the frost on the ground. When the sons of Israel saw it, they said to one another, "What is it?" For they did not know what it was. And Moses said to them, "It is the bread which the LORD has given you to eat. This is what the LORD has commanded, 'Gather of it every man as much as he should eat; you shall take an omer apiece according to the number of persons each of you has in his tent.'" The sons of Israel did so, and some gathered much and some little. When they measured it with an omer, he who had gathered much had no excess, and he who had gathered little had no lack; every man gathered as much as he should eat.

Exodus 16:13–18

Jesus believed that this account of the manna in the wilderness was quite important. In fact, in John 6 we find him giving a sermon right out of Exodus 16. The entire chapter is worthy of further consideration, but we will focus on John 6:48–51.

> I am the bread of life. Your fathers ate the manna in the wilderness, and they died. This is the bread which comes down out of heaven, so that one may eat of it and not die. I am the living bread that came down out of heaven; if anyone eats of this bread, he will live forever;

and the bread also which I will give for the life of the world is My flesh.

(John 6:48–51)

What was Jesus's point? "Your [fore]fathers ate the manna in the wilderness," he said, "and they died." In other words, *that* manna did not, ultimately, save anyone. Yes, it prolonged physical life. Yes, it was a great blessing to hungry bodies. But it was not, ultimately, meant to sustain anyone's *soul*. The people were not to be satisfied simply because they were Israelites and thus had the unique privilege of eating this bread that had never been seen before and has never been duplicated since. They could do all those things and still die in their sins. So the manna—refreshing and miraculous as it was—was not an end in itself. God gave it as a prelude to something more important (John 6:51). The manna was just a symbol—a portrait—of a far better, far more satisfying, longer-lasting kind of bread.

"The manna in the wilderness, the bread that rained down from heaven," Jesus was saying to the crowds, "was a picture of God's ability to provide sustenance and satisfaction, not just for your bodies, but also for your souls. Indeed," he said, "the manna was actually a portrait of me! That miraculous bread was a symbol! But I am the reality. Your fathers ate the manna in the wilderness, and they died. But I am the living bread that came down out of heaven; if anyone eats of *this* bread, he will live forever."

"This is the bread which comes down from heaven—my

flesh," Jesus said. And it is no accident that, when God's provision came down in the person of his Son, it came down in a place called Bethlehem, whose name means "house of bread." So, from Exodus 16 (which I hope you will read in its entirety), let us walk through the parallels between the manna in the wilderness and the manna God sent that holy night in Bethlehem. Observe, first of all, that both Jesus and the manna in Exodus 16 were:

Necessary bread

Notice the grumbling that stirred in the Israelite camp at the end of Exodus 16:3: "you have brought us out into this wilderness to kill this whole assembly with hunger." We will comment later on the ugliness and ungratefulness of their murmuring. But for now, simply notice the reason *why* the Israelites grumbled. I do not believe that the people were exaggerating when they said they were hungry. They should not have complained about it, to be sure, but it does appear that they were telling the truth.

You may remember that, in the previous chapters, God had rescued these Israelites from slavery in the land of Egypt. But their exodus from that country meant a long, hard march through the wilderness. The only food they would have carried would have been whatever non-perishables they could load onto their carts and stuff into their saddlebags. So we do not wonder that now, forty-five days into their wilderness wanderings (see 16:1), the rations were becoming quite slim.

The people really were hungry! And, if God did not provide

some sort of sustenance, they would all have died right there in the desert floor within the first few weeks of their marvelous deliverance from Egypt. Food—and, in this case, miraculously provided food—was an absolute necessity. There were no wheat fields, no vegetable gardens, no fruit groves—and no prospects for planting any of the above—in the Sinai wilderness. So miraculous provision was an absolute must. And God *did* provide. "I will rain bread from heaven," he told Moses in verse 4. And so he did—six days a week for forty years.

That "bread from heaven" was the Israelites' salvation. It was absolutely necessary. And, as we have been saying, that "bread from heaven" was carved in the likeness of Jesus. For is not Jesus absolutely necessary to *us*? Is it not true that, without Jesus, men, women, boys, and girls—each reader of these pages included—will die in the wilderness? Not a physical wilderness, of course. But, as Isaiah the prophet wrote, "your iniquities have made a separation between you and your God" (Isaiah 59:2). Your sins have driven you into a spiritual wasteland where God is not—and where you will perish unless God sends a miracle of manna in the wilderness. And he has! Christ is that manna! For, though you are separated from God, "Christ ... died for sins once for all, the just for the unjust, so that He might bring us to God" (1 Peter 3:18). Christ died for sins—and for sinners—so that he might bring you back out of the wilderness; so that he might keep you from dying; so that he might sustain your soul and bring you to God. And without him, you perish—and so do I.

So the bread in the wilderness—in its absolute necessity—is a portrait of Jesus. Jesus is our manna from heaven! Have you eaten yet?

Consider a second parallel between Jesus and the manna from heaven. Both were:

Undeserved bread

A fact that stands out most obviously and miserably in Exodus 16 is the Israelites' whining about their lack of food. In verse 2 we read that "the sons of Israel grumbled against Moses and Aaron." More significantly, Moses reminded the people in verse 8 that their grumblings were not against himself, mainly, "but against the LORD." For God was the one who had undertaken to provide for them. God was the one who had led them into the wilderness in the first place. And so God was the one they were really complaining against. And they had no right! God had just delivered them from the most brutal form of slavery. He had poured out his plagues on the cruel Egyptians. He had made them to walk through the midst of the Red Sea on dry ground. And, just in the previous chapter, he had miraculously provided water for them in the middle of the desert!

The Israelites were blessed. They had no right to complain! Yet complain they did. And when they were not complaining, they busied themselves by disobeying God's clear, concise instructions. He told them not to save any of the manna overnight (16:19), but in verse 20 we find them doing the exact opposite. He told them not to gather bread on the Sabbath day (v. 26), but in verse 27 we discover that "some of the people went out to gather" on the Sabbath.

The point of this record of complaining and disobedience is to show that the people were absolutely undeserving! God would have been well within his rights, after all their murmuring and defiance, to have withdrawn the manna from them. Given their sorry attitudes, it would not have been unjust for him never to have sent it in the first place. But he did send it! The manna was not simply necessary bread, it was also undeserved bread!

So, once again, we have in Exodus 16 a perfect portrait of the gospel. For Jesus came into the world to save, not deserving people, but undeserving ones! "It is not those who are healthy who need a physician, but those who are sick" (Mark 2:17). That is the good news! God sends manna from heaven to undeserving people. That was true of the world into which God sent Jesus, in the flesh, two thousand years ago, and it is true as Jesus comes to us in the gospel today.

Every moment of our lives, God has upheld us. He is the one who makes the grain to grow so that we can have bread. He is the one who gives us bodily strength so that we can earn money to buy that bread. He is the one who has given us friends and family to enjoy. He is the one who has allowed us to live in a land where books like this are not banned and burned. Indeed, it is God who gives us the very air we breathe. Yet you so often forget him—and so do I. You so often murmur about your circumstances—and so do I. You so often find yourself doing the exact opposite of what he has commanded—and so do I.

We are all just like the Israelites: immensely blessed, and not nearly reciprocal in our thanksgiving and obedience toward the Giver of all good things. In fact, we are often downright rebellious. But God, in his unparalleled mercy, has sent his Son to us anyway! He has demonstrated his love for us "in that while we were yet sinners, Christ died for us" (Rom. 5:8). God has sent "the living bread" to those who do not deserve it!

Not only has God granted us necessary and undeserved bread, but he has also given us:

Enough bread

"When they measured it with an omer, he who had gathered much had no excess, and he who had gathered little had no lack; every man gathered as much as he should eat" (Exod. 16:18). In other words, the bread was enough! In fact, God made a provision so that, on the day before the Sabbath, there would be twice as much bread—enough to cover the people's needs for two days (vv. 22 and 29)! So the point is clear: God's provisions for his people were sufficient! There was never any lack. No one died of starvation for those forty years in the wilderness. No one ever had to add to or supplement what God had provided. He gave them enough!

And what a wonderful parallel Exodus 16 provides of the sufficiency of Jesus. He is enough! His blood is sufficient to cover all your sins. His flesh, which he gives as bread for the life of the world (John 6:51), is sufficient to rescue you completely from dying in the wilderness. You will never have to add anything to it. You will never have to supplement the finished work of Christ with anything of your doing—not trying harder and doing better; not works of penance to help cancel out some grievous sin; not a certain amount of money placed on the offering plate. None of that is necessary! Jesus has already done everything that needed to be done to make amends for all your ungratefulness, forgetfulness, and rebelliousness against the Lord. He is absolutely, positively *enough* to save you from all your sins!

He is enough in other ways, too. If you had no other friend or comforter, Jesus would be enough. If you had no other counsel, his Word would be enough. If you had no one else to talk to, you could always talk to him. He, like the daily manna in the wilderness, is enough!

True, we do not always *feel* that Jesus is enough. Our hearts seem always to long for something more, something better, something newer, something more tangible. But the Israelites were like that, too. That is why some of them gathered more bread than they needed and stored it away for the next day's breakfast. They were not sure—at the beginning at least—that the daily bread would be enough. But, as time went on, I do not doubt that many of them learned, "I don't need anything more than what God has provided. When I am hungry again tomorrow morning, God will still be there to meet my needs." May it be that we learn the same lesson as we grow in grace! It should be our prayer that the older we get, and the more we experience, the more we will realize that Jesus really *is* all we need; that he really is enough; that we really can rejoice and be content without so many of the things that we once thought we could not live without. Jesus is enough!

God also provides us with:

Sweet bread

When we emphasize the sufficiency of the manna in the wilderness—that no one had too much and no one had too little—we must be careful that we do not imagine that God made his people live on war rations, or that he gave them just enough daily calories to barely keep them alive. That is not the picture that Exodus 16 presents. When the text emphasizes that God gave them just enough, it does not imply that the people's diets were in any way meager, bland, or merely utilitarian. Indeed, verse 31 tells us that the manna God provided tasted like "wafers with honey"! In other words, the bread that God provided was both sufficient and lavish; utilitarian but also delicious; nourishing and necessary, but also sweet and luxurious!

Is that not just like God? In providing for our needs, he never intends that we become greedy or bloated. But he does not usually give us war rations, either! He gives us just what we need, yes. But he often puts a dollop of sweetener on top! This is especially true when we think about the provision that he has made for us in the gospel. Yes, Jesus is necessary. Yes, he is sufficient. Yes, he accomplished a goal that is, in some ways, utilitarian—the forgiveness of our sins. We could not survive without that. But we should not think of Jesus as a mere wafer that fully, but blandly, satisfies our need for spiritual nourishment!

The good news is not just that our spiritual *need* has been met, but that our need has been met in such a way that we can *enjoy* it! Jesus is certainly like a wafer that satisfies our need and keeps us alive, but the wafer is spread with honey! For Jesus has not merely provided the forgiveness of sins, he has also promised to be our friend; he has brought us into a family—the family of God; he has allowed us to know God as Father; and he has lavished love on us at every turn.

The gospel is not a mere utilitarian message—useful and necessary as it is; the gospel is a wafer *coated with honey*! It provides for our needs, and does so in the sweetest way possible. Jesus is not just bread, but sweet bread! Are you enjoying him as such? Are you reveling in his friendship, in his love, in your newfound ability to call God Father? Are you regularly tasting and seeing that the Lord is good—in his Word, in prayer, in song? Is Jesus sweet to your taste? Or just useful?

Reflect on these points

1. *Which of the four parallels between the manna in the wilderness and Jesus, "the bread of life," is it most necessary for you personally to absorb? Is it your great need of Jesus and the forgiveness he provides? Or perhaps the undeserved nature of this provision? Is it the sufficiency of Jesus for every situation in your life? Or the sweetness of Jesus as Friend and Lover of your soul?*

Think about how God is speaking to you through the bread that came down out of heaven, and embrace what he is saying.

2. *In John 6, Jesus pushed the manna symbol to what many of his contemporaries felt was an extreme when he said, "unless you eat the flesh of the Son of Man and drink His blood, you have no life in yourselves" (v. 53). What do you think he meant by "eating" his flesh and "drinking" his blood? What did he not mean? Have you done what he asks you to do in that verse?*

3. *Another parallel between Jesus and the manna in Exodus 16 is the miraculous nature of both. The manna has no precedent or scientific explanation—it can only be understood as a miracle. How does the miraculous nature of the bread picture Jesus? To start with, take a close look at the incarnation accounts in Matthew 1–2 and Luke 1–2.*

The tabernacle
in the
wilderness

Then the LORD spoke to Moses, saying ... "Let them construct a sanctuary for Me, that I may dwell among them. According to all that I am going to show you, as the pattern of the tabernacle and the pattern of all its furniture, just so you shall construct it."

Exodus 25: 1, 8–9

"In the beginning was the Word," says the apostle John of Jesus in the very first verse of his Gospel, "and the Word was with God, and the Word was God." "All things came into being through Him" (John 1:3). "In Him was life" (v. 4). "And," astoundingly, "the Word became flesh, and dwelt among us" (v. 14). It is breathtaking enough to think that the Word—the eternal God himself (v. 1)—would become "flesh," but it is even more so when we discover that, in becoming flesh, he came to dwell among sinners like us!

But there is more treasure to mine from John 1:14. For the phrase "and dwelt among us" is more literally translated "and *tabernacled* among us."[1] The word "tabernacle" (to pitch one's tent) is not an everyday word in modern English—which is, perhaps, why all the major English Bible translations speak of Jesus *dwelling*, rather than *tabernacling*, among us. But it is helpful to understand this literal translation of John 1:14 because the word "tabernacle" has a rich significance in biblical history.

The tabernacle was a holy tent God commanded Moses and the Israelites to build and furnish in Exodus 25–30. It was the place where the people offered *sacrifices* for sin, where God promised to make his *dwelling*, and where God promised to *meet* with his people. So when John 1 tells us that Jesus "tabernacled" among us, we learn not only about his incarnation—that God himself, in the person of Jesus, came to dwell with mankind (as all the English versions make clear)—but also that, when Jesus came to dwell among us, he was *tabernacling* among us. There are other Greek words meaning "dwelt" which John could have used, but he chose this peculiar word, "tabernacled." Why? So that we might recognize that *Jesus* now fulfills all the roles the tabernacle had once performed, and that the Old Testament tabernacle was meant to be a foreshadowing, or portrait, of Jesus.

The tabernacle, and the more permanent temple that replaced it (see 1 Kings 5–9), pointed forward to something greater, and John 1:14 reminds us of that fact. The tabernacle was actually a portrayal of Jesus, a Christ-revealing tapestry woven in fine linen, scarlet thread, silver, and gold. For, ultimately, Jesus, not the lambs offered at the tabernacle, is the *sacrifice* for our sins; the fullness of God now no longer *dwells* in the tabernacle but in Jesus (Col. 2:9); and Jesus, not the tabernacle, is, now and forever, the *meeting place* between God and man!

The tabernacle (with its entire surrounding complex) was God's elaborate, ornate, and very deliberate picture of his Son! In this chapter, our aim is to look at this picture more closely from Exodus 25–30, hoping to see as much of Jesus as we can.

A sketch of the tabernacle complex

At this point it may help if you read Exodus chapters 25–30
in their entirety—particularly if you are not familiar with the
scale and plan of the tabernacle complex. The sketch may also
prove helpful.

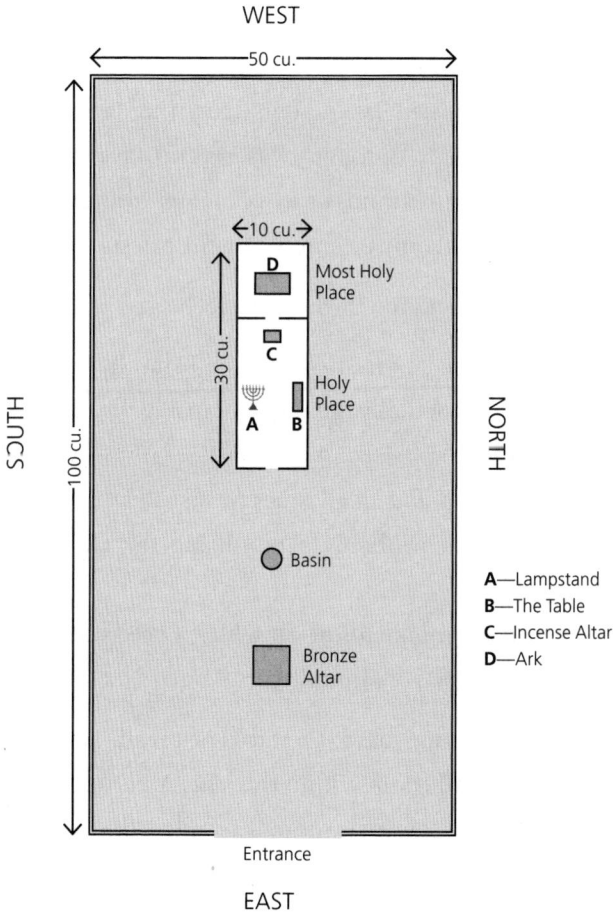

GROUND PLAN OF THE TABERNACLE

As a priest entered the courtyard from the east, he was confronted with three items:

- *a bronze altar*, where animals were slain and offered up in fire as sacrifices of atonement for the sins of the people;
- *a bronze laver* (or water basin), in which the priests were to wash themselves before beginning their duties;
- *the holy tent itself.* This tent (the "holy place," the "tabernacle" proper) was several layers thick, made from various kinds of woven material and animal hides, and could only be entered by the priests themselves.

As the priest entered the holy place, he saw:

- *a golden candlestick* (or lampstand), which was to burn perpetually, giving light inside the otherwise dark room;
- *a golden table*, at all times furnished with twelve loaves of bread, probably symbolizing the twelve tribes of Israel;
- *a small golden altar*, on which sweet-smelling incense was burned continually.

Beyond the lampstand, the table of bread, and the incense altar was a small room within the tent. A perfect cube (fifteen feet on all sides), this little room was called "the holy of holies" (sometimes "the most holy place"). It was in this most holy place, on top of a golden chest called the "ark of the testimony" (or "ark of the covenant"), that the presence of God dwelled in a cloud of smoke (Exod. 40:34–35). That was why it was "most holy"—because God dwelled there. And into that tiny room, where God made his dwelling, only the high priest could enter—and that only once a year and with the blood of the sacrifice in his hands for the forgiveness of the people's sins and also his own (see Lev. 16).

A purposeful pattern

It should be noted that this holy tent, with all its accoutrements, was not built with mere functionality or aesthetics in mind (beautiful and useful as it was). It would appear, rather, that each item (and its placement) was meant to correspond to some detail in God's heavenly throne room. For Moses was given a visual "pattern" from which to work (Exod. 25:9, 40), and the author of Hebrews seems to indicate that the pattern Moses saw was, in fact, cut from heavenly fabric. Hebrews 9:11 and 24 tell us that there is a true and more perfect tabernacle in heaven, and that the earthly tabernacle was fashioned as a "copy" of that "true" tabernacle. So every detail in the tabernacle was important. This tent was meant to be a picture of heavenly realities!

Every item in and feature of the tabernacle, therefore, had some spiritual significance.[2] Some details were meant to remind the people of the holiness and beauty of God; others pointed to the ugliness of sin and man's need for forgiveness. The lampstand, the prophet Zechariah tells us, was a symbol of the Holy Spirit (Zech. 4). But, as the author of Hebrews says about the tabernacle, "of these things we cannot now speak in detail" (Heb. 9:5). There were, however, not a few features of the tabernacle that were meant as foreshadowings of the Messiah himself, as portraits of Jesus.

Let us go on a scriptural tour of the tabernacle grounds, looking at three items in particular which pointed very clearly to Jesus and to his gospel. We will look at these articles in the order in which a worshipper would have encountered them when entering the tabernacle complex. Let us begin just inside the linen fence, with:

The bronze altar

The first item that a worshipper encountered when making his or her way through the entrance of the courtyard was the bronze altar. Made of wood and overlaid with bronze, the altar was 7.5 feet square and 4.5 feet tall (see Exod. 27:1–2). One might almost picture it (I say this reverently) as a large charcoal grill, since, below the top ledge, there was a bronze grate under which a fire could be kindled (27:4–5).

According to chapter 29, this altar was to be the place of animal sacrifice—specifically, of the sacrifices that were necessary to atone for human sin. Bulls, goats, rams, sheep, and other animals were slain at the doorway of the courtyard and then their bodies were offered up in fire on the bronze altar.

So the altar of bronze, and the sacrifices made there, were a constant reminder to the people of their sinfulness, of their need for atonement and forgiveness, and, most significantly, of God's provision of atonement and forgiveness. Thus, it was no accident that the altar was just inside the doorway of the courtyard. Before worshippers could get anywhere near the tent where God dwelt, they were forced to remember their need for forgiveness; they were reminded that God may only be approached when a sacrifice has been made for sin—a fact which remains true today.

But the author of Hebrews reminds us that "it is impossible for the blood of bulls and goats to take away sins" (Heb. 10:4). He reminds us that the tabernacle, with its bronze altar and animal sacrifices, was not an end in itself. These things were merely symbols. They were like charcoal sketches of the true and effective atonement that God himself would make for his people—through the blood of his own Son! We have been "brought near" (Eph. 2:13), not by goats' blood, but "by the blood of *Christ*." If we desire to enter the courts of God, Christ our sacrifice is the first thing we see—Christ, the "lamb unblemished and spotless" (1 Peter 1:19); Christ, who willingly shed his blood for our sins; Christ, "the Lamb of God who takes away the sin of the world" (John 1:29).

So the bronze altar standing between the worshipper and God's presence, and the animals that were slain on it, were portraits of Jesus and of his cross! Therefore, the tabernacle and its altar beg the question, have *you* been brought near to God "by the blood of Christ"? If so, then you are ready to move past the altar and toward:

The tent itself

Viewed from the outer courtyard, the holy tent—the tabernacle itself—was the centerpiece of the complex. And John 1:14 tells

65

us that the tent was also a portrayal of Jesus. How so? The following are the two most obvious ways.

THE EXCLUSIVITY OF JESUS

As you read the tabernacle blueprints in Exodus 25–30, it becomes clear that there was always only one way in. The outer fence contained only one doorway. Similarly, the holy tent contained a single doorway. The same was true of the most holy place within the tent. All three doorways were covered with blue and scarlet veils. This is instructive! God was reminding his ancient people that there are not many different ways to God; the door into his presence is shut unless we come to him on his terms.

What was the prescribed way of coming into God's presence? Through the one doorway, through the veil, and always with blood in the priest's hands to atone for sin. The way to God *was* open, there *was* a doorway in, but there was only *one* doorway, and a covered one at that. And all this symbolized that God may be approached, but not in a "come as you please" kind of way.

Do we not find the same situation in the New Testament? Entry into God's presence is still limited to those who will come on his terms. There is still only one way to meet with God—through Jesus, who "tabernacled among us" (John 1:14). As the author of Hebrews puts it, "we have confidence to enter the holy place by the blood of Jesus, by a new and living way which He inaugurated for us *through the veil*, that is, *His flesh*" (Heb. 10:19–20).

Yes, we have access to God, but there is still a veil. The doorway is not flung completely open. We cannot come to God any way we like. He may not be known through Mohammed, or the Buddhas, or the visions of Joseph Smith. Nor can we buy a ticket into God's presence by means of good works or local-church membership. There is still only one way of access to the Father: "through the veil, that is, [Jesus's] flesh." Jesus said in John 14:6, "*I* am the way ... no one comes to the Father but through Me."

THE INCARNATION OF JESUS

Notice from Exodus 25:8 that the "sanctuary," or tabernacle, was constructed so that God might "dwell among them." Indeed, we read in Exodus 40 that, when the construction was complete, God made his presence visible in the holy of holies in the form of a cloud. God himself came and lived in the tabernacle! There is certainly mystery in that fact. How can the God of the universe, who cannot be contained by the heaven of heavens, come and dwell in a 225-square-foot room? We can't say exactly how it worked. But it did!

God literally dwelt among his people in that tent! And Exodus 25:8 ("that I may *dwell among* them") sounds an awful lot like John 1:14, which tells us that Jesus "became flesh, and *dwelt among* us." Now we understand why John thought of Jesus's flesh as a tabernacle: because Jesus, in his flesh, was doing for his New Testament people exactly what God had done for the saints of the Old Testament—dwelling, or tabernacling, among them!

So the tabernacle is a portrait of Jesus, a foreshadowing of what would come: God dwelling among his people in the person of his Son! Again we ask, How can this be? How could the God of the universe confine himself to a human body? As with God's dwelling in the tent, we cannot explain all the details, but it happened! "[T]he Word became flesh, and [tabernacled] among us"!

Finally, that Word-made-flesh is portrayed in the tabernacle by means of:

The ark of the covenant

We could spend an entire chapter admiring the ways in which the ark of the covenant points us to Jesus. I trust that you will read Exodus 25:10–22 and do some thinking on this subject yourself. But, for the purposes of this chapter, let me simply point out that the ark of the covenant portrayed Christ in each of his offices of Prophet, Priest, and King.

CHRIST AS PROPHET

In Exodus 25:22 we are told that, from his place above the ark of the covenant, God promised to speak to his people. So the ark was the place from which the people expected to hear from God. They looked to the tabernacle, and specifically to the ark, when they needed a word from on high. But "in these last days [God] has spoken to us *in His Son*" (Heb. 1:2). When *we* need a word from on high, we turn to Jesus as we encounter him in the Scriptures. Jesus is our ark! He is God's Word to his people! God says of him what he said of the tabernacle in the wilderness: "There I will meet with you" and there "I will speak to you" (Exod. 25:22)—in Jesus. Are you listening?

CHRIST AS PRIEST

The ark of the covenant was the place where the blood of atonement was sprinkled, in God's presence, on behalf of the people. Yes, the blood of the animal sacrifices was shed at the tabernacle's outer doorway, beside the bronze altar (Exod. 29). But Leviticus 16 informs us that, on one particular day of the year, the blood of atonement was brought behind the veil by the high priest and sprinkled onto the lid (or "mercy seat") of the ark. The blood was brought into the very dwelling place of God so that he could see it and be satisfied; so that he could remember his promise to forgive the people's sins. So the ark became a symbol, not only of God's meeting with and speaking to his people, but also of his forgiving them. And, once again, we find that all that the ark promised was fulfilled in Jesus. Hebrews 9:23–25 reminds us that Jesus, acting both as sacrifice and as high priest, also took blood—his own blood— into the very presence of God so that we might be forgiven! Have *you* received his high-priestly ministry on *your* behalf?

CHRIST AS KING

God's presence dwelled, in a cloud of glory, above the ark (Exod. 25:22)—like a king on his throne. Indeed, Hebrews 9 seems to indicate that the tabernacle was a replica of God's heavenly throne room. So God dwelled in the midst of his people, in glory (Exod. 40:34–35) and as their King. But where does God demonstrate his glory and his kingly authority today? No longer in a cloud above the ark of the covenant, but in his Son! In Exodus 40:35, "the glory of the LORD filled *the tabernacle*." But in John 1:14, the glory of the Lord filled the tabernacle of Jesus's flesh! Isn't that what John says? "The Word became *flesh,* and [tabernacled] among us, and *we saw His glory*"! Do you see the parallel John is making between Jesus and Exodus 40? The glory of God is still on display, but in a different tabernacle! Just as Moses and the Israelites saw God's glory in the cloud, so John saw it even more clearly in the person of Jesus. The very same God whose glory filled the tabernacle in Exodus 40 was now dwelling with his people again—as a glorious King—in the flesh of his Son! Have *you* seen his glory? And is he *your* King?

Reflect on these points

1. Exodus 25:23–30 describes the table of showbread, or the "bread of the Presence"—twelve loaves (likely symbolizing the tribes of Israel) continually set out before the Lord in the tabernacle. Consider what God might have been saying to the people by having all twelve tribes represented before him in this way. How does this correspond to our being "in Christ"?

2. It has been said that the tabernacle is the most complete of all the Old Testament portraits of Jesus. It may also be the most complex. Think about and study the furnishings and plans that have not been covered in this chapter, and ponder how they too may point to Jesus.

See the suggestions for other resources on the tabernacle provided in the endnotes of this book.

3. *If we summarized the parallels we have drawn between Jesus and the tabernacle, we might say that the tabernacle pictures Jesus's sacrifice, his incarnation, his exclusivity, and his authority (as Prophet, Priest, and King). Which of these aspects of Christ's person do you struggle most to embrace (in faith or practice)? What sorts of service, commitments, questions, or cries for help is God perhaps spurring you to offer through what you have read?*

The serpent
on a pole

*Then they set out from Mount Hor by the way of the Red
Sea, to go around the land of Edom; and the people became
impatient because of the journey. The people spoke against
God and Moses, "Why have you brought us up out of Egypt
to die in the wilderness? For there is no food and no water, and
we loathe this miserable food." The LORD sent fiery serpents
among the people and they bit the people, so that many people
of Israel died. So the people came to Moses and said, "We have
sinned, because we have spoken against the LORD and you;
intercede with the LORD, that He may remove the serpents
from us." And Moses interceded for the people. Then the LORD
said to Moses, "Make a fiery serpent, and set it on a standard;
and it shall come about, that everyone who is bitten, when he
looks at it, he will live." And Moses made a bronze serpent and
set it on the standard; and it came about, that if a serpent bit
any man, when he looked to the bronze serpent, he lived.*

Numbers 21:4–9

This incident took place in the middle of Israel's forty
years of wandering in the Sinai wilderness awaiting
entrance into the Promised Land. It had not been enough for
the Israelites that God had rescued them from slavery in the
land of Egypt, provided miraculous safe passage across the
Red Sea, given them manna from heaven so that they did not
have to work for their food, and now (in Num. 21:1–3) had
heard their prayer and protected them from the onslaught of
the Canaanites. Even after all these deliverances and blessings
(and many others, too), the people of God still murmured
against him. Listen, in the ears of your mind, to a three-year-

old's whine: "I'm hungry! I'm thirsty! I don't like this food! Waaah!" and you probably have some idea of what Numbers 21:5 must have sounded like in God's ears!

How did the Lord respond? By sending poisonous snakes ("fiery serpents") that bit the people so that many of them died (v. 6). That may seem like a drastic repayment for a little whining about food. But when you consider all that God had done for his people—and all the complaining, disobedience, and idolatry that they had thrown his way in return—we can well understand why God was righteously indignant. And it is the same with us, is it not? When we consider that God created us; that he gives us the very air we breathe; that he has given us food, clothing, family, and every good thing—our rebellion against him is no small thing. We, too, the apostle Paul reminds us, deserve "death" (Rom. 6:23).

Death because of sin—and excruciatingly painful death, too! That was the mess in which the people of God found themselves in Numbers 21:4–6. But this was also the dark-hued background behind the bright portrait of his Son that God was about to paint. And it is truly a portrait of Jesus, and of the gospel, that we find brushed onto the canvas of Numbers 21:7–9! That is what Jesus himself tells us in John 3:14–15: "As Moses lifted up the serpent in the wilderness, even so must the Son of Man be lifted up; so that whoever believes will in Him have eternal life."

As we reflect on the Father's gospel portrait in Numbers 21, and Jesus's explanation of it in John 3, we will be helped by considering the account of the bronze serpent under four headings:[1]

A likeness

Notice carefully what God required Moses to hang up on the pole—a "serpent." But not just any serpent. When the people cried out to God for mercy (v. 7), God commanded Moses to "Make *a fiery serpent*, and set it on a standard" (v. 8). So there was *a likeness* involved in God's remedy for the people's sin, a likeness or replica of the "fiery serpents" that God had sent as a judgment upon their sin (v. 6). That is surely why Moses made it out of bronze (v. 9)—so that, when the sun shone in the sky, the bronze would radiate and glow, almost like a flame, making the snake look almost exactly like the fiery, poisonous serpents that had bitten the people.

These similarities between the bronze serpent and the poisonous ones are quite significant. Why was God so concerned that the serpent on the pole would look precisely like the "fiery serpents" which he had sent among the people in verse 6? Perhaps as a sign that the fiery poison that was in the serpents (and in the people) had been dealt with—crucified, if you will. The brazen color of the snake symbolized that it was a *poisonous* snake, and that the poison itself had therefore been hanged too!

Is this not a remarkable picture of what happened when Jesus was "lifted up" on his "standard"? It wasn't just that a man died on a cross. It wasn't even simply that a very good (indeed, sinless) man died on a cross. It was that the sinless man who died on the cross had actually taken deadly poison up there with him. Not the poison of a venomous snake, of course, but the deadly poison of *sin*. For Paul tells us that the Father made Jesus "who knew no sin to *be* sin on our behalf" (2 Cor. 5:21). As he went to the cross, the poison of sin went with him, literally, in just the same way it had been symbolically hanged with the brazen serpent in Numbers 21.

So it wasn't just that a man died on the cross, but that, for everyone who believes, the poison of sin died with that man! Sin can no longer kill or master the person who looks to Jesus! That is good news! And, as we turn our attention back to Numbers 21, we are reminded that God wants that good news published everywhere—which brings us to our second heading.

A lifting

God instructed Moses not only to make a bronze serpent, but also to "set it on a standard." If you have ever gone to a battle reenactment or watched a medieval war movie, you know what a standard is: a large flagpole that carries a king or army's insignia, conspicuously announcing the army's approach, might, and identity. Today we might think of the American flag or the Union Jack flying high atop a naval warship. That is a standard—a long pole that holds up a message for all to see. And that is where Moses was to hang this brazen symbol of healing—up on a pole, in the middle of the camp, where everyone could see it.

God wanted all the people to know that there was a remedy

for their sins and sufferings! And, says Jesus in John 3:14, "As Moses lifted up the serpent in the wilderness, even so must the Son of Man be lifted up." Jesus was also placed on a standard of sorts—on a cross in a major city, on the town garbage heap where everyone could see him. This is what Paul means when he says that Jesus was, by his Father, "displayed publicly as a propitiation" (Rom. 3:25). God wanted everyone to see the remedy for sin. And, through the preaching of the gospel extending into the remotest parts of the earth, God still wants Jesus "displayed publicly"; God still wants everyone to see the remedy for sin. The gospel is for people "from every tribe and tongue and people and nation" (Rev. 5:9).

So, just like the serpent lifted up on a pole, Jesus has been and is being lifted up for all to see—in the pain of Golgotha and in the preaching of the gospel. And just as with the serpent (v. 9), "any man" who looks to Jesus will be forgiven and live eternally—a fact which brings us to our third heading.

A looking

Moses had to go to the trouble of tracking down the bronze, crafting the snake, constructing a standard, and putting it all together. But did you notice how simple the remedy was for the people? They did not have to contribute anything to the bronze fund, or sculpt their own snake, or perform any religious ritual, or make any grand promises. Their part was actually quite easy: "it shall come about, that everyone who is bitten, *when he looks* at [the serpent], he will live."

"When he looks … he will live"! That was it! Just look and

live! That was God's simple message to the people. And aren't the instructions we receive in the gospel just as straightforward and generous? We, too, must simply look to Jesus and live. We do not have to have a religious professional pronounce something over us. We do not have to pay anything. We need not add anything to the remedy that God has provided, or come up with a solution on our own. We need not make God grandiose promises of all that we will do for him if he will only forgive our sins. Not for a moment. Forgiveness of sins and the eternal life that comes with it are free, unmerited gifts! We need only look to Jesus—and live forever!

Jesus said it himself in John 3:14–15: "As Moses lifted up the serpent in the wilderness, even so must the Son of Man be lifted up; so that whoever believes will in Him have eternal life." Whoever looks to ("believes in") the Son will live! It is so simple!

It must have seemed a bit ridiculous to some of the Israelites when Moses hung up the piece of metal in the middle of the camp and said, in effect, "If you are bitten by a poisonous snake, just turn your eyes upon this bronze replica and God will heal the snakebite." In the same way, it seems naïve and simplistic to some today when someone says to them, with no moral or religious strings attached, "Believe in the Lord Jesus Christ and you will be saved" (see Acts 16:31). That is why Jesus stresses that we must "believe" (John 3:15). What he means is that the kind of looking God blesses is a look of faith; a look that says, "God said 'Look at the snake,' so I'm going to look at the snake," or "God said 'Look to my Son,' so I am going to look to his Son." That is what God wants from us—a look of faith. The kind of look that says to Jesus, "My eyes are fixed on you alone. I have no other solutions. Indeed, your solution is not the one *I* would have come up with or thought clever. But I'm just going to trust you to heal me, as you have said, with no caveats, qualifications, or small print."

Have you looked to Jesus in that way—believing that he really is God's remedy for all that ails you? Believing that it really is that simple? If not, will you do so this very moment? The bronze serpent has, as it were, been lifted up before your eyes in this chapter. Indeed, Jesus has been placarded before you continuously for the last five chapters of this book, so you have surely caught a glimpse of him. But will you really *look* to Jesus now? Will you trust in him as the Savior of sinners? "[E]veryone who is bitten, when he looks at [Jesus], he will live."

Those last three words—"he will live"—summarize our fourth and final section.

A living

"[I]t came about, that if a serpent bit any man, when he looked to the bronze serpent, *he lived*" (v. 9). That is straightforward, is it not? If you looked to the brazen serpent, trusting God's promise, the venom was counteracted, the swelling went down, and you lived. That is simple enough, but it is also profound. The serpents that were poisoning the people did not slither into the Israelite camp by accident. It was not as

79

though a change in climate or the sudden presence of people and animals in the desert now made the Israelite camp an ideal haven for poisonous snakes. No, the serpents had been sent as a direct judgment from God!

The people of Israel, just like men and women today, were dying, not mainly because of the serpents (in the case of the Israelites), but because of their sins. And that puts a whole new spin on things when we read that God provided a remedy! God was not, in Numbers 21, like the modern physician who is under oath to help anyone who is sick; God was actually the one who made these people sick. And justly so! Therefore, he did not have to heal them or let them live.

So when we read that "if a serpent bit any man, when he looked to the bronze serpent, he lived," we are reading about something greater than what happens when, in a rural town, a boy gets bitten by a viper and is saved because the local doctor happens to have the right antivenin in his storage closet. Wonderful as that kind of healing is, there is far more going on in Numbers 21. These people were not just getting antivenin for accidental snakebites; they were being forgiven for sins which deserved death! And in that way, this passage, once again, points us to the gospel of Jesus. For what happens when we look to Jesus and gain eternal life is not simply that we do not have to die forever, and that we get to go to heaven. Those things are true. But there is far more to the gospel than simply being able to say, "I'm so glad I don't have to die and go to hell." What makes that so amazing is that death and hell are exactly what we deserve!

It would be one thing if God provided antivenin for a boy who got bitten because he was simply in the wrong place at the wrong time. That would be marvelous! But it is far more amazing, and merciful, and loving when God provides antivenin for a man, woman, boy, or girl who has got bitten, not because he or she went out into the woods where the snakes are, but because God himself sent the snakes into his or her house as a deadly punishment for sins. And that is what we have in Numbers 21, and in the gospel of Jesus. People who deserve to perish forever and ever—who deserve eternal damnation—instead get "eternal life"! And all they have to do is "look" to Jesus!

"[E]veryone who is bitten" (and all of us are, by sin) "when he looks at [Jesus]" (and any of us may, today) "*will* live."

Reflect on these points

1. *Have you looked to Jesus, trusting him as the one and only remedy for your sins? Really? If not, what is it that is keeping you from doing so? Will you give to God whatever it is that is holding you back, and entrust yourself to Jesus today?*

2. *There are ways in which people, every day, look at Jesus without being healed. Looking at him incredulously, or as a necessary but uninspiring part of the Sunday routine, is not the kind of looking that God blesses in Numbers 21 and John 3. Are there ways in which you*

81

regularly see Jesus without really looking to him in faith?

3. *Are you involved in God's ongoing public display of Jesus? Yes, he was lifted up, once for all, at the cross. But are you, like Moses, willing to lift up God's remedy for sin in whatever camp God has placed you? At work? At school? Across the fence in your backyard? With your children? And is the character and quality of your life a kind of "standard" in itself?*

The lover
of our souls

May he kiss me with the kisses of his mouth!
For your love is better than wine.
"Your oils have a pleasing fragrance,
Your name is like purified oil;
Therefore the maidens love you.
Draw me after you and let us run together!

Song of Solomon 1:2–4

How many of your non-churchgoing friends would believe it if you told them that there is a book of the Bible which begins with the phrase, "May he kiss me with the kisses of his mouth"? Perhaps not many! But the Song of Solomon begins in exactly this way (1:2). Verse 1 is, in effect, just the title page of this most unusual portion of Scripture, but the text of the song actually begins in verse 2, with a young woman longing for a kiss! And if you think that seems odd and un-church-like, just keep reading! The language only gets more passionate as you go along!

This little-known book, the Song of Solomon, is actually a long love poem exchanged between King Solomon and a young village girl who had become his bride. Here is another extract that helps us gauge the temperature of the book; this time, we read Solomon's words for his bride:

> How beautiful are your feet in sandals,
> O prince's daughter!
> The curves of your hips are like jewels,
> The work of the hands of an artist.
>
> (7:1)

You can understand why it was an ancient Jewish saying that the Song should not be read by anyone under the age of thirty![1] The book is filled, not with graphic or lewd expressions, but certainly with intimate and romantic ones. For that reason, it has a great deal to teach married couples about romance, intimacy, and true love. But, as we saw with Abraham's faith in Chapter 2, we should see more in the Song of Solomon than our own reflection. The love that is depicted in this book is also meant to teach us something about our Savior!

The apostle Paul reminds us that, amid all its other joys and pleasures, the most noble purpose of holy matrimony is that it can and should serve as a reflection of the love that passes back and forth between Christ and his people (Eph. 5). Marriage is an everyday gospel portrait! Therefore the Song of Solomon, the Bible's book of marriage, surely has something to teach us—not only about marriage itself, but also about the far greater love that exists between Jesus and his church! Consider three ways in which Solomon's Song depicts the love between Christ and the church.

The king was in love

It is important to remember that this love poem was written by and about a king. And not just any king: Solomon is described in the Bible as the most powerful, resplendent, and the wisest of all the kings of the ancient world. Listen to how he is depicted in chapter 3 of the Song:

What is this coming up from the wilderness
Like columns of smoke,
Perfumed with myrrh and frankincense,
With all scented powders of the merchant?
Behold, it is the traveling couch of Solomon;
Sixty mighty men around it,
Of the mighty men of Israel.
All of them are wielders of the sword,
Expert in war;
Each man has his sword at his side,
Guarding against the terrors of the night.
King Solomon has made for himself a sedan chair
From the timber of Lebanon.
He made its posts of silver,
Its back of gold
And its seat of purple fabric,
With its interior lovingly fitted out
By the daughters of Jerusalem.

(3:6–10)

That was Solomon, king of Israel! So it was no small thing for this village lass to say in 1:4, "*The king* has brought me into his chambers." *The king* was in love with her. Not a good-looking young man from the village; not a leader in the community; not the son of the chief elder; not even one of the valued and esteemed priests of Jerusalem. The man who had fallen for her was *the king* himself!

Young girls today often squeal, giggle, and swoon at the

mere thought of the captain of a football team *noticing* them, much less desiring to court them! But what must it have been like for *the king*—in this case, the most powerful man, not only in the country but in the entire world—to have asked this young girl to marry him, and to have brought her "into his chambers"?

Far more exhilarating is to think what it means that the King, the Creator of the universe, the only begotten Son of God, the Ruler of all the earth, the Savior of the world, wants to have a relationship with *us*; wants *us* to be his bride; wants to betroth himself to *us*! Have you thought about that? Have you put yourself in the shoes of the young girl in the Song of Solomon? Or the seventeen-year-old schoolgirl? Do you get butterflies in your stomach when you realize that the King's phone number is, as it were, on your caller ID? That he wants to spend time with *you*? That he wants a lifelong relationship with *you*?

Can you turn down the King when he asks for your hand in marriage? When he offers you an eternal life of friendship and love? When, after the betrothal, he wants to continue spending quality time with you daily? Those who are still outside of Christ need to ponder those questions seriously. The King has invited you to be his very own! Can you refuse him? Can you make him wait even one moment longer while you weigh the pros and cons? Surely you cannot! Surely today is the day to say "yes" to him!

The King is in love! Indeed, you may find even more motivation to receive his love when you consider that:

The king loved a simple girl

Some commentators identify Solomon's "darling" as the daughter of Pharaoh, whom Solomon did marry, it would appear, in younger days. This assumption is made because she is called a "prince's daughter" (7:1), and because of her noticeably dark skin (1:5). But, interestingly, the young maiden in this love song is not called an Egyptian but a "Shulammite" (6:13). It would appear, then, that she was from the small town in Galilee sometimes called Shunem and other times called Shulem. The reason why she was so dark-skinned, therefore, was not because she was African, but because, as she said in 1:6, "the sun has burned me. My mother's sons were angry with me; they made me caretaker of the vineyards."

So the picture this book paints of Solomon's bride is that of a rural farm girl. Presumably Solomon called her a "prince's daughter" because he appreciated her stately bearing and regal manner. But she was, in point of fact, a simple (though bright and lovely) small-town girl who spent her days working her parents' grape farm. The German commentator Franz Delitzsch describes her brilliantly:

> The range of her thoughts is not that of a king's daughter, but of a rustic maiden ... She is from the country; she is dark-complexioned ... from the open sunshine to which she has been exposed as the keeper of

a vineyard; in body and soul she is born to be a princess, but in reality she is the daughter of a humble family in a remote part of Galilee; hence the child-like simplicity and the rural character of her thoughts, her joy in the open fields, and her longing after the quiet life of her village home [see, for instance, 7:10–13].[2]

This background information is certainly interesting. But why is it important? That a king should marry a pretty girl from a small town certainly makes for good storytelling. Anyone who has ever read Cinderella knows that! But why take such time on it in these pages? Simply because it is a perfect illustration of how Jesus found *us*, and why he loved us.

We were (and are) not loved by God because of some innate greatness. He did not set his affections upon us because we were born royalty, or born great, or even because we, somewhere along the line, achieved greatness. The apostle Paul wrote to the church at Corinth, "consider your calling, brethren, that there were not many wise according to the flesh, not many mighty, not many noble" (1 Cor. 1:26). And he could have written those words to nearly every gathering of Christians that may be found on planet earth. The church is made up, almost wholly, of normal, run-of-the-mill folk. In fact, we could often describe ourselves as a bit ragtag. And even when some son or daughter of privilege or might does join our numbers, it is still true that God does not love him or her on account of position or acumen.

The King is in love with simple, normal people. He does

not ask us to be great. And he certainly does not ask us to be worthy of his affection. Like Solomon's love for the small-town girl from Galilee, God's love is for people who are far beneath him.

Is that not good news—that the King of the universe is not afraid to offer his hand to small-timers? That the King is not averse to loving commoners like us? That the King has not allowed the vast chasm between his stature and ours to keep him from loving us?

And here is the best part: it is not that we, like Cinderella, had to pretty ourselves up and appear to be something we really are not so that the King would notice us. No, in this real-life, gospel fairytale, it is not *Cinderella* who goes where *she* does not fit in so as to be noticed by the King and win his heart; it is *the King* who first notices Cinderella—in the person of spiritual paupers like you and me—and goes where *he* does not fit in to win her hand! In 2 Corinthians 8:9 we are reminded that "though He was rich, yet for your sake He became poor." Though he was rich, he came and dwelt among the common folk in a Galilean town not all that far from Shunem. Though he was rich, he actually took on flesh and became one of the townspeople—one of us—so that he might take us to be his beloved bride!

The King loves those who are far beneath him! And, even more amazing:

The king was willing to die for love

In chapter 8 we read,

> Put me like a seal over your heart,
> Like a seal on your arm.
> For love is as strong as death,
> Jealousy is as severe as Sheol;
> Its flashes are flashes of fire,
> The very flame of the LORD.
> Many waters cannot quench love,
> Nor will rivers overflow it;
> If a man were to give all the riches of his house for love,
> It would be utterly despised.
>
> (8:6–7)

The text does not clearly indicate exactly who spoke these lines—Solomon or the Shulammite. But, regardless of who spoke them, the sentiment conveyed is a profound one. Solomon and his bride believed that "love is as strong as death" and that "If a man were to give all the riches of his house for love, it would be utterly despised." In other words, love is so powerful that those who truly have it are willing to give up everything they own—and consider it nothing—for love's sake. A man who truly loves his wife is willing to sell his entire estate and give away his entire fortune in order to keep her. Indeed, he would be willing to give up his very life for her. For "love is as strong as death."

Apparently, this was the kind of love that passed between Solomon and the Shulammite. He was willing to give up everything for her—even to die for her. Thus the Song of Solomon once more provides us with an astonishing picture of

Jesus. For if anyone could ever say "Amen" to those verses, it was Jesus! He actually went through with it. When he left his Father's throne and came to walk upon this guilty earth, he did indeed "give all the riches of his house for love." And when he carried his cross to the place Golgotha and laid down his life there, he proved that love truly is "as strong as death."

Jesus Christ was willing to die for us! That is how much he loves sinners! Indeed, he told us that "Greater love has no one than this, that one lay down his life for his friends" (John 15:13).

To be sure, we do not always *feel* that Jesus loves us. Circumstances do not always go the way we had hoped. Prayers are not always answered in the way we thought. Difficulties can arise. Bible reading can seem cold. Prayer may be perfunctory. So we may sometimes find ourselves asking, "Jesus, do you really love me?" But, in those dark moments, we need only look to the cross to remember his love. If he gave us no other evidence of his love, we would know that it was real by looking to the cross and remembering that "love is as strong as death."

The king—not just Solomon, but Jesus too—was willing to die for love. Indeed, the King *did* die for love! Do you believe it? Have you allowed yourself to receive his love? Have you responded, like the Shulammite, by loving him in return?

Reflect on these points

1. *One of the most obvious themes of the Song is the*

beauty that Solomon saw in his bride (see especially chs 4, 6, and 7). Given our sinfulness, it would seem that the analogy between the Song and Christ and his church would break down at this point, for we certainly are not beautiful in our sins. But think about how, in spite of the ugliness of sin, the king's love for a beautiful girl might also be a gospel portrait. Look specifically at Ephesians 5:22–33.

2. *It was not simply that Solomon loved the Shulammite; she was quite enamored with him, too! Reread the Shulammite's speaking parts in the Song. How do they challenge you in your love toward Christ?*

3. *The Song is a picture of Jesus and the church. But it is also, at a more basic level, a picture of healthy romance and marriage. Read the book with your spouse and ask yourself how your marriage might better reflect the health and joy that existed between Solomon and his bride.*

The sign of Jonah

The word of the LORD *came to Jonah the son of Amittai saying, "Arise, go to Nineveh the great city and cry against it, for their wickedness has come up before Me." But Jonah rose up to flee to Tarshish from the presence of the* LORD. *So he went down to Joppa, [and] found a ship which was going to Tarshish ... The* LORD *hurled a great wind on the sea and there was a great storm on the sea so that the ship was about to break up. Then the sailors became afraid ... [Jonah] said to them, "Pick me up and throw me into the sea. Then the sea will become calm for you, for I know that on account of me this great storm has come upon you" ... So they picked up Jonah, threw him into the sea, and the sea stopped its raging. ... And the* LORD *appointed a great fish to swallow Jonah, and Jonah was in the stomach of the fish three days and three nights.*

Jonah 1:1–5, 12, 15, 17

A s Jesus went about preaching, healing, befriending sinners, forgiving sins, and claiming to be the Son of God, many of his countrymen (especially among the leading classes) were jealous and incredulous. So, in spite of all the evidence that seemed to flow from him at every turn, they asked him to prove himself again and again. "Do another miracle and then we will believe you," was the tenor of their reaction toward him.

So what was Jesus's response to the constant skepticism?

He answered and said to them, "An evil and adulterous generation craves for a sign; and yet no sign will be given to it but the sign of Jonah the prophet; for just as Jonah was three days and three nights in the belly of the sea monster, so will the Son of Man be three days and three nights in the heart of the earth. The men of Nineveh will stand up with this generation at the judgment, and will condemn it because they repented at the preaching of Jonah; and behold, something greater than Jonah is here.

(Matt. 12:39–41)

He pointed his detractors to "the sign of Jonah," who spent three days and three nights buried and left for dead. "Just like him," says Jesus, "I also will be buried three days 'in the heart of the earth.' Watch for it! That will be your sign!" And a powerful sign it would be. For, if Jesus was to spend only three days and three nights in the heart of the earth,[1] *resurrection* was implied! So, though his hearers probably did not really grasp what he was saying, Jesus's response to the demand for miraculous signs was, "After I have spent three days buried in the heart of the earth, I will, like Jonah, rise again. Will you believe in me then?"

This is a remarkable statement. Jesus's response reminds us that the resurrection is *the* sign, *the* evidence, *the* beyond-the-shadow-of-a-doubt proof that Jesus was certainly not a religious phony with a Messiah complex. In addition, the resurrection demonstrates that Jesus was not *just* a good teacher, miracle-worker, or prophet. Many good teachers, prophets, and even miracle-workers have come onto the world stage, but none of them woke him- or herself from the sleep of death! Jesus, however, "was declared the Son of God ... by the resurrection from the dead" (Rom. 1:4). The importance of the sign of Jonah—of Jesus spending three days and three nights in the heart of the earth and rising again—is that it demonstrates him to be "the Son of God"!

That is why Jesus pointed to this one sign in particular. "Do you remember what happened with Jonah?" he says to his critics. "Three days and three nights in the belly of the fish ... and then, all of a sudden, he reappeared! You're going to see it again—only this time, far more amazingly. And when you do, you will know that I am who I have been claiming to be: 'the Son of God.'"

Jonah's burial and resurrection is another Old Testament snapshot of Jesus in at least three different ways.

The reason for the burial

Jesus and Jonah were both buried and left for dead—Jonah "in the belly of the sea monster" and Jesus "in the heart of the earth." But, although they were buried in different locations, they were both buried for the same reason—as a punishment for sin.

This fact is clear in the book of Jonah. The reason why "the LORD appointed a great fish to swallow Jonah" and why he "was in the stomach of the fish three days and three nights" in Jonah 1:17 was because, in Jonah 1:3, "Jonah rose up to flee to Tarshish from the presence of the LORD." It was because of his sin. Even Jonah himself understood this (1:12). There *is* a penalty for sin—both a chastisement, meant to discipline us and get us back on the right track, and a final penalty for those who refuse to repent. It seems that Jonah, in the stomach of the fish, was hanging in the balance between the two. He was being punished, and even buried, because of his sin, but, thankfully, Jonah repented and was rescued before the punishment became final.

So Jonah was buried (albeit temporarily) as a punishment for sin. And when we turn to the New Testament we realize that Jesus was buried in the heart of the earth for the very same reason. But not for his own sin. For, as Peter tells us, Jesus "committed no sin" (1 Peter 2:22). Rather, Jesus was buried in the heart of the earth for Jonah's sin—and for yours and mine. That, ultimately, is why Jonah did not have to stay in the belly of the great fish or go to hell for fleeing from the presence of the Lord—and why you and I do not have to, either, if we believe. God was sending (and has now sent) a sacrifice: a Savior who would die and be buried for the sins of the world; who would come and take upon himself the punishment that we all deserve!

So it was for one and the same reason that Jesus and Jonah found themselves buried—as a punishment for sin. But Jesus faced the far more severe punishment; indeed, a punishment that was not his own but was one that you and I have earned. Never forget that. Our sins are worthy of death. But God, in his infinite mercy, buried his Son in the grave that Jonah deserved. You and I deserve that grave, too. Make sure that you, like Jonah, repent (Jonah 2:9) and receive that provision of forgiveness!

Next we notice a similarity between Jonah and Jesus when it comes to:

The length of the burial

This is the most obvious connection of all, and Jesus states it clearly in Matthew 12:40: "just as Jonah was three days and three nights in the belly of the sea monster, so will the Son of Man be three days and three nights in the heart of the earth."

The exact correspondence of the days is clearly meant to give us the "wow" effect. In other words, had Jonah risen from his burial after one day, and Jesus after three, we might be a little bit impressed with the connection between the two, but the fact that they were both buried exactly three days makes us say to ourselves, "This is surely no coincidence. These stories line up exactly. It must have been the same compassionate and gracious God working in the life of Jesus as was saving sinners eight hundred years before through the preaching of Jonah. Jesus must have been not merely a charismatic religious trendsetter, but a man sent by divine appointment!"

The exact correspondence between Jonah's burial and that of Jesus is simply too much to chalk up to coincidence. That is what Jesus was saying to his critics in Matthew 12: "If the miracles themselves do not convince you, do a little study of the Old Testament and see if you are not amazed at how much of it is being precisely replayed right before your eyes."

I would say the same thing to anyone who has questions

about the authenticity of the Bible or the truthfulness of the claims of Jesus. It is simply unthinkable that so many Old Testament prophecies could have come exactly true in the life and ministry of Jesus unless the Bible really is divine and Jesus really was (and is) who he said he was. It is unimaginable that so many Old Testament events could so precisely mirror the life and ministry of Jesus simply by chance.

The whole Bible—written over the span of a couple of millennia—fits together like a perfectly cut jigsaw puzzle. And it has been the purpose of these chapters to demonstrate that, when all the pieces are in place, the image that comes together quite clearly is the face of Jesus. These gospel portraits did not come about by accident! Rather, the seamless and unified nature of the tapestry which the Scriptures weave together is a testament to their divine character and trustworthiness. The exact correspondence between Jonah's burial and that of Jesus is simply further proof.

Now notice a third (and most vital) parallel between Jonah and Jesus:

The resurrection after the burial

We are not sure what exactly went on for those three days that Jonah was in the stomach of the great fish. Some scholars believe that he actually died. He spoke about descending "to the roots of the mountains" and of having "the earth with its bars ... around [him] forever" (Jonah 2:6). This sounds like a reference to death. Other scholars hear Jonah praying in 2:7 and repenting in verse 9 and conclude that he did not actually die, but that his death language in verse 6 indicates that he was as close as one can possibly imagine to doing so; that he was, in fact, certain that this would have been his fate if God had not intervened.

Whatever position you take on the question, one thing is sure—Jonah was certainly not, as the children's books often depict him, sitting inside the fish's rib cage waiting patiently and singing hymns! He was either dead or as good as dead. He would have nearly drowned, having been thrown overboard in a raging storm. He would have had very little oxygen—and no food or drink—for three solid days. The fish's digestive juices would surely have already begun to work upon him. So, whether those fluids actually finished Jonah off or not, it was going to take a miracle for Jonah to come out of the fish alive. And that is exactly what Jonah 2:10 records: one of God's greatest miracles—the resurrection of Jonah!

And once more we have, in the narrative of Jonah, a picture of Jesus! The only difference is that, in Jesus's case, the New Testament writers make it very clear that he did actually die. There is none of the unclear language that we find in Jonah 2. The Roman soldiers, who dealt with death every single day, did not break Jesus's legs to speed up the process of death because—experts that they were—they clearly saw that Jesus was already dead (John 19:31–33). Therefore, as in the case of Jonah, the latter chapters of each of the four Gospels record *a miracle*—God's greatest miracle; the miracle upon which the entirety of Christianity hinges; the miracle without which "[our] faith is ... vain" (1 Cor. 15:14)—the resurrection of Jesus Christ from the dead.

It must be said again that the whole point of Matthew 12:39–41, the reason for Jesus's fulfillment of the sign of Jonah, and the purpose of his rising from the dead, was to give *proof*! If we are not convinced by the resurrection of Jesus Christ—prophesied and foreshadowed in the Old Testament and verified with many convincing proofs in the New—what will convince us? But if we accept the veracity and miraculous nature of the resurrection of Jesus from the dead, then we can push all doubts aside!

Think on these things. Ask yourself, do I really believe that Jesus rose from the dead? And, if I do, is there any reason for me to doubt all the other good and miraculous things that God promises in his Word? Surely if I can believe in the resurrection, I can believe that God will fulfill, on my behalf, all his less spectacular promises of intervention—about my future, my finances, my suffering, my eternity, and so on!

If, on the other hand, you struggle with believing the reality of Jesus's resurrection, do some serious study and thinking. Ask yourself if the explanation and evidence given by the apostles is convincing, and if the arguments of modern-day skeptics are really as bullet-proof as they claim. Ask yourself whom you would rather trust—Jesus's contemporaries (both believing and unbelieving), who treated the resurrection, respectively, as either a glorious truth or a regrettable reality (but a reality nonetheless); or men and women who speculate from a distance of two millennia?

"The sign of Jonah"—given in Jonah 2 and fulfilled in the resurrection of Jesus—is among the most important truths in the universe. What you do with it is the most important decision you will ever make.

Conclusion

How shall we conclude these pages? By saying again that *the Old Testament really is all about Jesus.* It all points forward to him—sometimes in direct prophecy; sometimes by reminding us of our sin and the need for a Savior; sometimes through hints that a Messiah is coming; and sometimes in the form of *signs* (or *portraits*)—objects, people, and events that seem to mirror, hundreds of years in advance, the exact details of the life and work of Jesus! Jonah, who spent "three days and three nights in the belly of the sea monster," is just one of those portrait-signs!

In other words, when we read the book of Jonah—particularly the account of his three-day burial at sea—we are to think of Jesus. We are to recognize that, all along, God was preparing to send his Son. We are to see that strewn throughout the Old Testament are signs that, like breadcrumbs, lead us into the gospel accounts of Jesus's life and ministry. God was not only saving the Ninevites and the pagan sailors in the pages of Jonah; he was also charting the course of history so that, when Jesus appeared on the earth, we would have clear evidence that he fit right into God's plan; that the details of his life were too similar to those of the greatest Old Testament events to have happened by chance.

In these Old Testament gospel portraits, God has given us plenty of evidence that Jesus really was and is the long-awaited Messiah. The reason why Jesus's story sounds so much like the book of Jonah (and so much like the Passover lamb in Exod. 12, the ram in the thicket in Gen. 22, the serpent on the pole in Num. 21, the blueprints for the tabernacle in Exod. 25–30, and so on) is because God intended it that way—so that we would recognize the divine stamp on Jesus's life; so that we would recognize the Messiah when he came!

Do you recognize him? Is he your Messiah? Your Anointed One? Your hope? Your Savior?

Reflect on these points

1. *If there were another heading in this chapter, perhaps it would have been "The purpose of the resurrection." Reread Matthew 12:39–41 (and perhaps also Jonah 3). Why did God raise Jonah from the "dead"? What was to happen next? How does that parallel the purpose of Jesus's resurrection? What does it say to you, personally?*

2. *There are other gospel portraits in the book of Jonah. Read through the whole book and notice how many people came to repentance and faith when they were not at all looking for God! How does this parallel New Testament doctrine? How does it parallel your experience?*

3. *Think back through the various gospel portraits we have looked at, and their corresponding gospel truths and doctrines. Which portrait/truth has been most striking or moving for you? Why? How has your understanding of or appreciation for Christ and the gospel increased as you have read? Take a few moments and thank God for what you have seen of Jesus. As you pray, make (or remake) any commitments about which God has been stirring your heart.*

Endnotes

Introduction

1 Any emphasis given within scriptural quotations is the author's.

Ch. 2 The ram in the thicket

1 It should be noted that Abraham did have another son, Ishmael. But, because Ishmael was born illegitimately to Abraham's household servant, Isaac was considered the firstborn, indeed the "only son." In essence, Isaac was the only son of Abraham's marriage to Sarah; the only legitimate son.

2 See, for example, Ferguson's interview with Sovereign Grace Ministries: "God's Love for Us Displayed in the Cross (Ferguson Interview, pt 6)", April 1, 2008, at: sovgracemin.org.

Ch. 5 The tabernacle in the wilderness

1 R. V. G. Tasker, *The Gospel According to St. John (Tyndale New Testament Commentary Series*; 1960; 2000: Grand Rapids, MI: Eerdmans), p. 48.

2 For a more detailed but simple and Christ-centered study of the tabernacle and all its furnishings, I recommend the message series entitled "The Tabernacle" (January–April 2007) by the Rev. Kenneth Stewart (minister of Dowanvale Free Church, Glasgow, Scotland). These talks were very helpful to me in my studies and may be downloaded from the "Sermons" page on the Dowanvale Web site: dowanvale.org. Also helpful is Arthur Pink's *Gleanings in Exodus* (Chicago: Moody, 1972).

Ch. 6 The serpent on a pole

1 The first three points in this outline ("A likeness," "A lifting," and "A looking") I gleaned from "The Serpent of Bronze," a sermon on Numbers 21 by Rev. James MacIver of the Knock Free Church of Scotland (4 January 2009). The message can be accessed online at: knockfreechurch.co.uk/home.html. It was this sermon that inspired me to preach the sermon series that became this book!

Ch. 7 The lover of our souls

1 C. F. Keil and F. Delitzsch, and M. G. Easton, (tr.), *Commentary on the Old Testament, Volume 6: Proverbs, Ecclesiastes, and Song of Songs* (1866–1891; 2001: Peabody, MA: Hendrickson), p. 497.

2 Ibid. p. 499. Also see p. 585 for more information on the title "Shulammite" and the location to which it corresponds.

Ch. 8 The sign of Jonah

1 Because the New Testament makes it clear that Jesus was crucified on a Friday (see Mark 15:42 and Luke 23:54, where Jesus is said to have died on "the day of preparation," i.e. the day before the Saturday Sabbath), and because the New Testament is also clear that Jesus rose from the dead on a Sunday morning (see, for example, Luke 24:1), there is an apparent problem with Jesus stating that he, like Jonah, would be buried "three days and three nights": a Friday burial and Sunday morning resurrection would only allow for two nights in the tomb. A solution with which I tend to concur is to interpret "three days and three nights" as a generic and colloquial term that simply referred to a roughly three-day period. See R. T. France, *Matthew* (Tyndale New Testament Commentary; Grand Rapids, MI: Eerdmans, 1985), p. 213; and William Hendriksen, *The Gospel of Matthew* (Grand Rapids, MI: Baker, 1973), p. 534.

Also available

Pathways to peace
Facing the future with faith—
Meditations from Isaiah 40

JOHN KITCHEN

128PP, PAPERBACK

ISBN 978-1-84625-212-9

A million events assault the word tomorrow to make it the most uncertain word in the English language. As we stand at the threshold between a fretful past and a wishful future, what guarantee is there that tomorrow will be better than yesterday? Pathways to Peace sets forth the hope of Isaiah 40: Only God's presence sustains you in the panic of an uncertain future, and God's presence only helps you when you appreciate his preeminence over all things. Where God is lifted up as preeminent, he manifests his presence and the peace of God is the result in the believer's life..

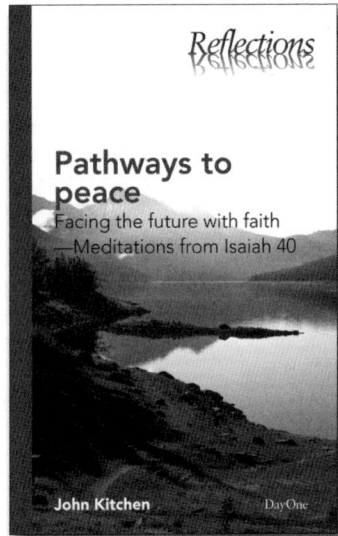

'John Kitchen's book on Isaiah 40 is a joy to read with its strong encouragement on how the preeminence and presence of our Lord affects all we do, think, and hope for as believers. I strongly encourage a wide usage of this book among all who need a spiritual uplift in these troubling days.'
WALTER C. KAISER, JR., PRESIDENT EMERITUS, GORDON-CONWELL THEOLOGICAL SEMINARY

'This is a refreshing and health-giving meditation on the grandest of all themes: the nature of God and how it affects our living today. It will strengthen your spiritual muscles and equip you to face the challenges you encounter victoriously.'
AJITH FERNANDO, NATIONAL DIRECTOR, YOUTH FOR CHRIST, SRI LANKA

On wings of prayer
Praying the ACTS way

REGGIE WEEMS

112PP, PAPERBACK

ISBN 978-1-84625-178-8

Constructing a prayer life is often like putting a puzzle together without the box's cover. Having a picture makes all the difference. Bible prayers create a model of what prayer can be; exciting, fulfilling and powerful. Using a simple acrostic makes prayer memorable, interesting and focused. You too can learn to pray following this simple outline utilized by men and women who experience the transforming power of prayer.

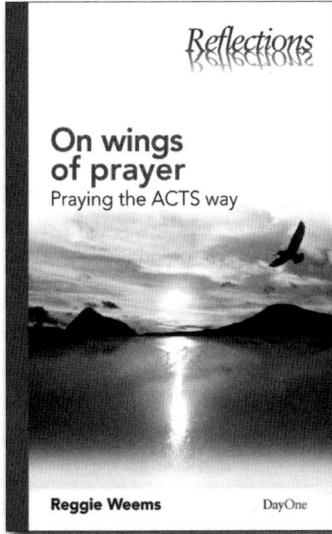

Reflections

On wings of prayer
Praying the ACTS way

Reggie Weems   DayOne

'This brief work on prayer will encourage you to pray, teach you to pray, and give you precious gems about prayer along the way. It taught me things I did not know, and reminded me of things I had forgotten.'
PAUL DAVID WASHER, HEARTCRY MISSIONARY SOCIETY

'Because of the unique nature of the Christian discipline of prayer, most books on prayer are more inspiring than they are helpful. Pastor Reggie Weems has achieved what only a few have ever done in Christian history. This book is orthodox, penetrating, motivating and inspiring, all in one slender, readable volume. If you are hoping to enhance your walk with the Master, here is one book that will bless your soul.'
PAIGE PATTERSON, PRESIDENT, SOUTHWESTERN BAPTIST THEOLOGICAL SEMINARY, FORT WORTH, TEXAS, USA

ABOUT DAY ONE:

Day One's threefold commitment:

- To be faithful to the Bible, God's inerrant, infallible Word;
- To be relevant to our modern generation;
- To be excellent in our publication standards.

I continue to be thankful for the publications of Day One. They are biblical; they have sound theology; and they are relevant to the issues at hand. The material is condensed and manageable while, at the same time, being complete—a challenging balance to find. We are happy in our ministry to make use of these excellent publications.

JOHN MACARTHUR, PASTOR-TEACHER, GRACE COMMUNITY CHURCH, CALIFORNIA

It is a great encouragement to see Day One making such excellent progress. Their publications are always biblical, accessible and attractively produced, with no compromise on quality. Long may their progress continue and increase!

JOHN BLANCHARD, AUTHOR, EVANGELIST AND APOLOGIST

Visit our web site for more information and
to request a free catalogue of our books.
www.dayone.co.uk

U.S. web site:
www.dayonebookstore.com